THE COMPLETE GUIDE TO FULL STACK WEB DEVELOPMENT

Learn to Build Scalable and Responsive
Websites with Modern Technologies

THOMPSON CARTER

TABLE OF CONTENTS

CHAPTER 24: BUILDING A SOCIAL MEDIA PLATFORM.......251

CHAPTER 25: FINAL CAPSTONE: BUILDING A SCALABLE SAAS APPLICATION 263

Introduction

The software development landscape has evolved tremendously over the past decade. The rise of modern technologies has made it possible to build sophisticated, scalable applications that address diverse business needs and customer expectations. Among these advancements, **full-stack web development** has emerged as a highly sought-after skill, enabling developers to bridge the gap between front-end user experiences and back-end functionality. This book, *The Complete Guide to Full Stack Web Development: Learn to Build Scalable and Responsive Websites with Modern Technologies*, is your definitive guide to mastering this art and craft.

Why Full-Stack Web Development?
In today's fast-paced, technology-driven world, the demand for developers who can create complete, end-to-end solutions is at an all-time high. Organizations are looking for professionals who can:

- **Design intuitive front-end interfaces:** Deliver responsive, visually appealing designs that engage users across devices.
- **Engineer powerful back-end systems:** Build robust server-side architectures to handle complex logic and data management.
- **Optimize performance:** Ensure applications are fast, reliable, and scalable to handle increasing demands.

- **Collaborate seamlessly across teams:** Understand the big picture and contribute effectively to both front-end and back-end processes.

Full-stack developers have the unique ability to integrate these elements into cohesive, functional applications, making them invaluable assets in the tech industry.

What This Book Offers

This book is designed for developers of all levels, whether you are a beginner taking your first steps in web development or an experienced programmer looking to expand your skill set into full-stack development. Here's what makes this guide unique:

1. **Comprehensive Coverage of Core Concepts:**
   o From foundational topics like **HTML, CSS, and JavaScript** to advanced frameworks like **React, Node.js, and GraphQL**, this book ensures you have a solid understanding of the tools and technologies that power modern web applications.

2. **Hands-On Learning:**
   o Each chapter includes practical examples, exercises, and real-world projects to help you apply what you've learned. By the end of the book, you'll have built several full-stack applications, including an e-

commerce website, a blogging platform, and a scalable SaaS application.

3. **Modern Best Practices:**

   o The book emphasizes best practices for coding, testing, and deploying applications, ensuring that you develop solutions that are secure, maintainable, and scalable.

4. **Focus on Scalability and Performance:**

   o In an era where applications must handle millions of users and vast amounts of data, scalability is key. This book dedicates entire sections to building architectures that can grow with demand while maintaining optimal performance.

5. **Integration of Cutting-Edge Technologies:**

   o Explore modern tools and techniques such as **microservices**, **serverless computing**, **real-time communication**, and **CI/CD pipelines** to build applications that are not only functional but also future-proof.

6. **Project-Based Approach:**

   o The capstone projects in this book combine all the concepts you'll learn, guiding you through the development of complex applications from scratch. These projects mimic real-world challenges, preparing you for a professional environment.

Who This Book Is For

- **Aspiring Developers:** If you're just starting your journey into web development, this book provides a clear and structured path to becoming a full-stack developer.
- **Front-End Developers:** Expand your skills by learning how to create back-end systems, manage databases, and handle server-side logic.
- **Back-End Developers:** Dive into front-end technologies to build user interfaces and understand the intricacies of delivering a seamless user experience.
- **Full-Stack Professionals:** Enhance your knowledge of the latest tools and trends to stay competitive in the ever-evolving tech landscape.

How This Book Is Structured

The book is divided into six parts, each focusing on a critical area of full-stack web development:

1. **Foundations of Web Development:** Covers the core building blocks like HTML, CSS, JavaScript, and version control with Git.
2. **Front-End Development:** Delves into advanced front-end techniques, including responsive design, React, and state management.

3. **Back-End Development:** Explores server-side programming with Node.js, database integration, RESTful APIs, and GraphQL.

4. **Advanced Full-Stack Concepts:** Introduces topics like authentication, performance optimization, and real-time communication.

5. **Scaling and Performance Optimization:** Focuses on deploying applications, building scalable architectures, and optimizing for performance.

6. **Full-Stack Projects:** Combines all concepts into hands-on capstone projects, including a SaaS application, an e-commerce platform, and a social media site.

What You'll Achieve

By the end of this book, you will:

- Have a deep understanding of the full-stack web development process.
- Be proficient in building responsive, interactive, and scalable applications.
- Understand how to integrate modern tools and frameworks into your workflow.
- Be equipped to tackle real-world challenges in full-stack development with confidence.

A Journey to Mastery

Becoming a full-stack web developer is not just about mastering technologies; it's about understanding how to think critically, design effectively, and code efficiently. This book is your companion on that journey. Whether you aspire to build innovative web applications, start your own SaaS business, or advance your career in tech, the skills you gain here will open countless opportunities.

So, let's get started. The future of web development is full-stack, and your path to mastery begins now.

Chapter 1: Introduction to Full Stack Development

Overview

Full stack development encompasses both the front-end and back-end aspects of web development, enabling developers to create complete, functional web applications from scratch. This chapter provides an overview of full stack development, detailing its scope, the role of front-end and back-end, and the skills and technologies required to excel in this field.

---

1. What is Full Stack Development?

Definition:

Full stack development refers to the development of both the **client-side (front-end)** and **server-side (back-end)** of a web application. A **full stack developer** has the expertise to work on both ends, ensuring seamless functionality and integration.

---

2. The Components of Full Stack Development

Front-End Development:

The front end is the **user-facing side** of a web application, where users interact with the interface.

- **Key Responsibilities:**
    - Designing layouts, buttons, menus, and other visual elements.
    - Ensuring responsiveness and compatibility across devices.
    - Implementing interactive features such as dropdowns, forms, and animations.
- **Core Technologies:**
    - **HTML (HyperText Markup Language):** Structures web content.
    - **CSS (Cascading Style Sheets):** Styles the content, including colors, fonts, and layouts.
    - **JavaScript:** Adds interactivity and dynamic behavior.

Back-End Development:
The back end is the **server-side logic** that handles data storage, processing, and communication with the front end.

- **Key Responsibilities:**
    - Managing databases and APIs.
    - Processing user inputs and serving responses.
    - Ensuring security and data integrity.

- **Core Technologies:**
  - **Programming Languages:** Python, Java, Node.js, Ruby, etc.
  - **Databases:** MySQL, MongoDB, PostgreSQL.
  - **Web Frameworks:** Express.js, Django, Spring Boot.

Full Stack Development:

Combining both front-end and back-end development, full stack development involves creating the entire application, from user interfaces to server-side logic and database interactions.

3. The Importance of Full Stack Development

1. **Versatility:**
   Full stack developers can work on both client and server sides, making them valuable assets to teams.
2. **Efficiency:**
   By understanding the entire stack, developers can ensure smoother integration between the front-end and back-end components.
3. **Career   Opportunities:**
   Full stack developers are in high demand due to their broad skill set and ability to handle diverse roles.

4. Key Skills for Modern Full Stack Development

Front-End Skills:

- **HTML5 and CSS3:** For structuring and styling web pages.
- **JavaScript (ES6+):** For dynamic content and user interactions.
- **Front-End Frameworks:** Knowledge of React, Angular, or Vue.js is essential for modern development.

Back-End Skills:

- **Server-Side Languages:** Familiarity with Node.js, Python, Ruby, or Java.
- **Databases:** Understanding relational databases (MySQL, PostgreSQL) and NoSQL databases (MongoDB).
- **API Development:** Ability to create and consume RESTful APIs or GraphQL.

DevOps Skills:

- **Version Control:** Using Git for collaboration and code management.
- **Deployment Tools:** Knowledge of CI/CD pipelines, Docker, and cloud services (AWS, Azure, Google Cloud).

Soft Skills:

- **Problem-Solving:** Ability to debug and resolve issues efficiently.
- **Communication:** Collaborating with team members and clients effectively.
- **Adaptability:** Keeping up with evolving technologies and frameworks.

---

5. Modern Technologies in Full Stack Development

1. **Front-End Frameworks and Libraries:**
   - **React.js:** A JavaScript library for building user interfaces.
   - **Vue.js:** A lightweight framework for progressive web apps.
2. **Back-End Frameworks:**
   - **Express.js:** A Node.js framework for building RESTful APIs.
   - **Django:** A Python framework for rapid web development.
3. **Databases:**
   - **Relational:** MySQL, PostgreSQL.
   - **NoSQL:** MongoDB, Firebase.
4. **Tools for Deployment and Collaboration:**
   - **Version Control:** Git and GitHub.

- o **Hosting:** Heroku, Netlify, AWS.

---

6. The Full Stack Development Workflow

1. **Planning:**
   Define project goals, user requirements, and features.
2. **Front-End   Development:**
   Create the UI/UX design and implement the interface using HTML, CSS, and JavaScript.
3. **Back-End   Development:**
   Set up the server, APIs, and database connections.
4. **Integration:**
   Connect the front-end and back-end to ensure data flows seamlessly.
5. **Testing:**
   Debug and test the application for functionality, performance, and security.
6. **Deployment:**
   Deploy the application to a live server and monitor its performance.

---

7. Real-World Applications of Full Stack Development

- **E-Commerce   Websites:**
  Platforms like Amazon and eBay rely on seamless integration between user interfaces and back-end systems.

- **Social   Media   Platforms:**
  Sites like Facebook and Twitter require robust front-end design and scalable back-end architectures.

- **Content   Management   Systems   (CMS):**
  WordPress and Drupal utilize full stack technologies to manage content and user interactions.

Full stack development offers a holistic approach to web development, combining the art of crafting user-friendly interfaces with the science of building efficient, secure back-end systems. As businesses increasingly rely on web applications to connect with users, full stack developers play a crucial role in bringing ideas to life. This chapter sets the stage for a deep dive into the tools, techniques, and projects that will help you master full stack development and create scalable, responsive websites with modern technologies.

Chapter 2: Setting Up Your Development Environment

Overview

A well-configured development environment is the cornerstone of efficient full stack web development. This chapter guides you through installing essential tools like VS Code, Git, Node.js, and package managers. Additionally, it explores the differences between local and cloud-based development environments, helping you choose the setup that best suits your workflow.

---

1. Tools You Need for Full Stack Development

1.1 Visual Studio Code (VS Code)

Why   **VS**   **Code?**
VS Code is a lightweight, yet powerful code editor with extensive support for web development.

Steps to Install VS Code:

1. Go to VS Code Download.
2. Download the installer for your operating system (Windows, macOS, or Linux).
3. Follow the installation prompts.

Essential Extensions for VS Code:

- **Prettier:** For automatic code formatting.
- **ESLint:** For identifying and fixing JavaScript issues.
- **Live Server:** For live previews of your front-end projects.
- **GitLens:** For enhanced Git integration.

1.2 Git

Why   Git?

Git is a version control system that allows you to track changes, collaborate with others, and manage your codebase efficiently.

Steps to Install Git:

1. Download Git from Git Download.
2. Run the installer and configure the options (use default settings unless required otherwise).
3. Verify installation:

   bash

   git --version

Basic Git Commands:

- **Clone a Repository:**

  bash

  git clone <repository_url>

- **Initialize a Repository:**

bash

git init

- **Add Changes:**

bash

git add .

- **Commit Changes:**

bash

git commit -m "Your commit message"

1.3 Node.js

Why   **Node.js?**
Node.js enables JavaScript to be run on the server-side and is essential for using npm (Node Package Manager).

Steps to Install Node.js:

1. Download the latest stable version from Node.js Official Site.
2. Install using the default settings.
3. Verify installation:

bash

```
node --version
npm --version
```

1.4 Package Managers

Why   Use   Package   Managers?
Package managers like **npm** and **yarn** simplify dependency management for your projects.

Install Yarn:

1. Run the following command:

   bash

   ```
   npm install -g yarn
   ```

2. Verify installation:

   bash

   ```
   yarn --version
   ```

---

2. Configuring Your Environment

2.1 Setting Up VS Code for Development

- **Themes and Settings:**

- o Customize your editor with themes from the marketplace.
  - o Configure auto-saving, code formatting, and other preferences in settings.json.
- **Integrating Git with VS Code:**
  - o Use the built-in Git features to commit, push, and pull changes.
  - o Open the Source Control tab to manage your repositories.

2.2 Creating a Project Directory

- Create a folder for your project:

bash

```
mkdir my-fullstack-project
cd my-fullstack-project
```

- Initialize a Git repository:

bash

```
git init
```

- Initialize a Node.js project:

bash

npm init -y

---

3. Local vs. Cloud-Based Development

3.1 Local Development
Advantages:

- Faster file access and operations.
- Full control over tools and configurations.
- No dependency on internet connectivity.

Challenges:

- Requires a powerful machine for resource-intensive tasks.
- Manual setup and configuration.

3.2 Cloud-Based Development
Overview: Cloud-based platforms like **GitHub Codespaces**, **Replit**, and **AWS Cloud9** provide online development environments that are preconfigured and scalable.

Advantages:

- Access your projects from anywhere.
- No setup required for complex tools and dependencies.
- Scalable computing resources for demanding tasks.

Challenges:

- Requires reliable internet access.
- Potential latency compared to local development.

---

4. Choosing the Right Setup

Feature	Local Development	Cloud-Based Development
Performance	High (depends on hardware)	Scalable
Flexibility	Full control	Limited by platform
Collaboration	Manual setup via Git	Built-in collaboration tools
Accessibility	Restricted to local device	Accessible from anywhere

Recommendation:

- Start with local development for full control and performance.
- Use cloud-based environments for collaborative projects or when working on multiple devices.

---

5. Testing Your Environment

Creating a Simple "Hello World" Application

1. Create a file named index.js in your project folder:

   javascript

   ```
   console.log("Hello, Full Stack Developer!");
   ```

2. Run the script:

   bash

   ```
   node index.js
   ```

3. Expected Output:

   mathematica

   ```
   Hello, Full Stack Developer!
   ```

Testing a Local Web Server

1. Install Express.js:

   bash

   ```
   npm install express
   ```

2. Create a simple Express server in server.js:

javascript

```javascript
const express = require('express');
const app = express();

app.get('/', (req, res) => {
    res.send('Hello, Full Stack Developer!');
});

app.listen(3000, () => {
    console.log('Server is running on http://localhost:3000');
});
```

3. Run the server:

bash

```bash
node server.js
```

4. Visit http://localhost:3000 in your browser to see the message.

Setting up your development environment is the first and most crucial step toward mastering full stack web development. By installing and configuring essential tools like VS Code, Git, and Node.js, you're building the foundation for a productive workflow. Whether you choose local or cloud-based development, ensure your setup aligns with your project needs and preferences. With your environment ready, you're now prepared to dive deeper into the technical aspects of full stack development.

Chapter 3: HTML Fundamentals

Overview

HTML (HyperText Markup Language) is the backbone of any web page, providing its structure and content. Understanding how to write semantic, accessible HTML is crucial for creating websites that are user-friendly, SEO-optimized, and compliant with web standards. This chapter introduces the fundamentals of HTML, focusing on semantic structuring, best practices, and enhancing web accessibility.

---

1. What is HTML?

Definition:

HTML is a markup language used to define the structure and content of web pages. It uses **tags** to specify elements such as headings, paragraphs, images, links, and more.

Basic HTML Structure:

html

```
<!DOCTYPE html>
<html lang="en">
<head>
    <meta charset="UTF-8">
    <meta name="viewport" content="width=device-width, initial-scale=1.0">
```

```
  <title>My First Web Page</title>
</head>
<body>
  <h1>Welcome to HTML Fundamentals</h1>
  <p>This is a basic HTML structure.</p>
</body>
</html>
```

---

2. Structuring Web Pages with Semantic HTML

What is Semantic HTML?

Semantic HTML uses meaningful tags to describe the purpose of content on a web page. It improves readability, accessibility, and SEO.

Common Semantic HTML Tags:

Tag	Purpose
<header>	Defines the header of a page or section.
<nav>	Specifies navigation links.
<main>	Represents the main content of a document.
<article>	Encapsulates a self-contained piece of content.
<section>	Groups related content within a page.

Tag   Purpose

<aside>   Represents complementary or sidebar information.

<footer> Defines the footer of a page or section.

<figure> Groups images or illustrations with captions.

Example: Semantic HTML Structure

html

```
<!DOCTYPE html>
<html lang="en">
<head>
  <meta charset="UTF-8">
  <meta name="viewport" content="width=device-width, initial-scale=1.0">
  <title>Semantic HTML Example</title>
</head>
<body>
  <header>
    <h1>My Website</h1>
    <nav>
      <ul>
        <li><a href="#home">Home</a></li>
        <li><a href="#about">About</a></li>
        <li><a href="#contact">Contact</a></li>
      </ul>
    </nav>
  </header>
  <main>
```

```
<section id="home">
  <h2>Welcome</h2>
  <p>This is the home section of my website.</p>
</section>
<section id="about">
  <h2>About Me</h2>
  <p>I am a passionate web developer.</p>
</section>
<aside>
  <p>Did you know? HTML was first introduced in 1991.</p>
</aside>
</main>
<footer>
  <p>&copy; 2024 My Website. All rights reserved.</p>
</footer>
</body>
</html>
```

3. Best Practices for Writing HTML

3.1 Use Descriptive Tags

- Choose tags that describe the content's purpose (e.g., use `<strong>` for emphasis instead of `<b>`).
- Avoid using `<div>` and `<span>` unnecessarily when semantic alternatives exist.

3.2 Validate Your HTML

- Use validators like <u>W3C Markup Validation Service</u> to check for syntax errors.

3.3 Indent and Organize Your Code

- Use consistent indentation and line breaks to improve readability.

3.4 Include Meta Tags

- Meta tags provide metadata about the web page.

  html

  ```
  <meta name="description" content="Learn HTML fundamentals for building websites.">
  <meta name="author" content="Your Name">
  ```

---

4. Accessibility Best Practices

Why Accessibility Matters

Accessible websites ensure that everyone, including individuals with disabilities, can interact with your content.

4.1 Use Proper Heading Levels

- Structure headings hierarchically:

  html

```
<h1>Main Title</h1>
<h2>Subsection</h2>
<h3>Sub-subsection</h3>
```

4.2 Provide Text Alternatives

- Add alt attributes to images:

html

```
<img src="image.jpg" alt="Description of the image">
```

4.3 Use ARIA Attributes

- Add ARIA (Accessible Rich Internet Applications) roles and attributes to enhance accessibility:

html

```
<nav aria-label="Main Navigation">
  <ul>
    <li><a href="#home">Home</a></li>
  </ul>
</nav>
```

4.4 Ensure Keyboard Navigation

- Test if all interactive elements (e.g., buttons, links) are accessible using only a keyboard.

5. Best Practices for SEO

5.1 Use Semantic Tags

- Search engines prioritize content wrapped in semantic tags.

5.2 Optimize Meta Tags

- Include relevant keywords in the title and description meta tags:

  html

  ```
  <title>HTML Fundamentals: Learn Web Development</title>
  <meta name="description" content="Master HTML fundamentals and
  build better websites.">
  ```

5.3 Use Descriptive Anchor Text

- Avoid vague anchor text like "click here." Use meaningful descriptions:

  html

  ```
  <a href="about.html">Learn more about us</a>
  ```

5.4 Optimize Images

- Compress images for faster load times.
- Use descriptive file names and alt text:

html

```
<img src="web-development-tips.jpg" alt="Web development tips illustration">
```

5.5 Use Header Tags Effectively

- Include target keywords in `<h1>` and `<h2>` headings to improve search visibility.

---

6. Common HTML Mistakes to Avoid

1. **Forgetting the DOCTYPE Declaration:**
   - Always include `<!DOCTYPE html>` at the top of your document.
2. **Using Deprecated Tags:**
   - Avoid outdated tags like `<font>` and `<center>`. Use CSS for styling instead.
3. **Improper Nesting:**
   - Ensure tags are nested correctly:

   html

   ```
   <ul>
     <li>Item 1</li>
     <li>Item 2</li>
   </ul>
   ```

4. **Missing Alt Attributes:**

   o   Always include meaningful alt attributes for images.

---

7. Practical Exercise: Building a Personal Profile Page

Objective:

Create a simple personal profile page using semantic HTML.

Requirements:

- Use <header>, <main>, and <footer> tags.
- Add a profile picture with a meaningful alt attribute.
- Include a section for hobbies and an aside for fun facts.

Example Starter Code:

html

```
<!DOCTYPE html>
<html lang="en">
<head>
  <meta charset="UTF-8">
  <meta name="viewport" content="width=device-width, initial-scale=1.0">
  <title>My Profile</title>
</head>
<body>
  <header>
    <h1>John Doe</h1>
```

```
      <p>Web Developer & Designer</p>
   </header>
   <main>
      <section>
         <h2>About Me</h2>
         <p>I am a passionate web developer who loves creating user-friendly
websites.</p>
      </section>
      <section>
         <h2>Hobbies</h2>
         <ul>
            <li>Coding</li>
            <li>Photography</li>
            <li>Traveling</li>
         </ul>
      </section>
      <aside>
         <p>Fun Fact: I have visited 20 countries!</p>
      </aside>
   </main>
   <footer>
      <p>&copy; 2024 John Doe. All Rights Reserved.</p>
   </footer>
</body>
</html>
```

HTML is the foundation of web development, and mastering its fundamentals is essential for building structured, accessible, and SEO-optimized websites. By focusing on semantic HTML, accessibility best practices, and SEO techniques, you can create web pages that are not only user-friendly but also aligned with modern web standards.

Chapter 4: CSS Basics and Responsive Design

Overview

CSS (Cascading Style Sheets) is the language used to style and visually enhance web pages, transforming basic HTML structures into visually appealing layouts. This chapter introduces CSS fundamentals, explores styling techniques, and delves into the principles of responsive design, including the use of media queries.

---

1. What is CSS?

Definition:

CSS is used to control the visual presentation of HTML elements, including their layout, colors, fonts, and more.

How CSS Works:

CSS can be applied to HTML in three ways:

1. **Inline CSS:** Directly within an HTML element.

   html

   This is blue text.

2. **Internal CSS:** Within a <style> tag in the HTML <head>.

html

```
<style>
  p {
    color: blue;
  }
</style>
```

3. **External CSS:** In a separate .css file linked to the HTML.

html

```
<link rel="stylesheet" href="styles.css">
```

---

2. CSS Syntax

Basic Structure:

css

```
selector {
  property: value;
}
```

- **Selector:** Targets the HTML element(s) to style.
- **Property:** Specifies the aspect of the element to style (e.g., color, font-size).
- **Value:** Defines the style to apply.

Example:

css

```
body {
    background-color: lightgray;
    font-family: Arial, sans-serif;
}
```

---

3. Styling Web Pages with CSS

3.1 Common Properties

- **Text and Font Styles:**

  css

  ```
  h1 {
      font-size: 2em;
      color: navy;
      text-align: center;
  }
  ```

  - font-size: Controls text size.
  - color: Sets text color.
  - text-align: Aligns text (e.g., left, center, right).

- **Box Model Properties:**

  css

  ```
  div {
  ```

```
width: 300px;
height: 200px;
padding: 20px;
margin: 10px;
border: 2px solid black;
}
```

- o   width and height: Set the size of the element.

- o   padding: Space between content and border.

- o   margin: Space outside the border.

- o   border: Defines the border style, width, and color.

- **Background Properties:**

css

```
body {
    background-color: #f0f0f0;
    background-image: url('background.jpg');
    background-repeat: no-repeat;
    background-size: cover;
}
```

- o   background-color: Sets the background color.

- o   background-image: Adds an image as the background.

- o   background-size: Specifies how the background image is displayed (e.g., cover, contain).

3.2 Selectors

- **Basic Selectors:**
  - o   h1 {}: Targets all <h1> elements.
  - o   #header {}: Targets an element with the id="header".
  - o   .nav {}: Targets all elements with the class nav.
- **Combinators:**
  - o   div p {}: Targets <p> inside <div>.
  - o   div > p {}: Targets <p> directly inside <div>.

---

4. Responsive Design Principles

What is Responsive Design?

Responsive design ensures that web pages look and function well on all devices, from desktops to smartphones.

4.1 Flexible Layouts
Using Relative Units:

- Use %, em, and rem for sizes to ensure flexibility.

css

```
div {
    width: 80%; /* Relative to the parent element */
```

```
padding: 1em; /* Relative to the font size */
}
```

CSS Grid and Flexbox:

- **Flexbox:** A layout module for creating flexible, row or column-based layouts.

  css

```css
.container {
   display: flex;
   justify-content: space-between;
}
```

- **Grid:** A powerful system for designing complex layouts.

  css

```css
.grid {
   display: grid;
   grid-template-columns: repeat(3, 1fr);
   gap: 10px;
}
```

4.2 Media Queries

What are Media Queries? Media queries apply CSS rules conditionally, based on device characteristics like width, height, and resolution.

Syntax:

css

```
@media (condition) {
    /* CSS rules */
}
```

Example:

css

```
/* Styles for screens wider than 768px */
@media (min-width: 768px) {
    body {
        font-size: 1.2em;
    }
}

/* Styles for screens narrower than 480px */
@media (max-width: 480px) {
    nav {
        display: none;
    }
}
```

5. Building a Responsive Web Page

Example: Responsive Page Structure

HTML:

html

```html
<!DOCTYPE html>
<html lang="en">
<head>
  <meta charset="UTF-8">
  <meta name="viewport" content="width=device-width, initial-scale=1.0">
  <link rel="stylesheet" href="styles.css">
  <title>Responsive Design</title>
</head>
<body>
  <header>
    <h1>Responsive Web Page</h1>
    <nav>
      <ul>
        <li><a href="#home">Home</a></li>
        <li><a href="#about">About</a></li>
        <li><a href="#contact">Contact</a></li>
      </ul>
    </nav>
  </header>
  <main>
    <section id="home">
      <h2>Welcome</h2>
      <p>Explore responsive design with CSS.</p>
    </section>
  </main>
  <footer>
    <p>&copy; 2024 Responsive Design Co.</p>
  </footer>
```

```
</body>
</html>
```

CSS:

css

```css
/* General styles */
body {
    font-family: Arial, sans-serif;
    margin: 0;
    padding: 0;
}

/* Header styling */
header {
    background-color: navy;
    color: white;
    padding: 20px;
    text-align: center;
}

/* Navigation styling */
nav ul {
    list-style: none;
    padding: 0;
    display: flex;
    justify-content: center;
}

nav ul li {
    margin: 0 15px;
```

```
}

nav ul li a {
    text-decoration: none;
    color: white;
}

/* Media Queries */
@media (max-width: 768px) {
    nav ul {
        flex-direction: column;
    }

    nav ul li {
        margin: 10px 0;
    }
}
```

---

6. Best Practices for Responsive Design

1. **Use the Viewport Meta Tag:**

   html

   ```
   <meta name="viewport" content="width=device-width, initial-scale=1.0">
   ```

2. **Design Mobile-First:** Start with styles for small screens and add media queries for larger devices.

3. **Test Across Devices:** Use browser developer tools or tools like BrowserStack to test responsiveness.

4. **Minimize Fixed Units:** Avoid using px for widths and heights; prefer relative units like %, em, or vw/vh.

5. **Optimize Images:** Use responsive image techniques:

html

```html
<img src="small.jpg" srcset="large.jpg 1024w" alt="Example image">
```

CSS is a powerful tool for creating visually appealing web pages, while responsive design ensures your site performs well on all devices. By mastering fundamental styling techniques, layout systems like Flexbox and Grid, and media queries, you can build scalable, responsive websites that provide a seamless user experience.

Chapter 5: JavaScript Essentials

Overview

JavaScript is a dynamic programming language essential for adding interactivity and dynamic behavior to web pages. This chapter covers the core concepts of JavaScript, including variables, data types, loops, and functions. It also introduces DOM manipulation and event handling, key skills for creating responsive and interactive websites.

---

1. Core Concepts of JavaScript

1.1 Variables

What are Variables? Variables store data that can be reused and manipulated in your program.

Declaring Variables:

javascript

```
let name = "John";   // Block-scoped variable
const age = 30;      // Constant, cannot be reassigned
var city = "London"; // Function-scoped variable (not recommended)
```

Key Points:

- Use let for variables whose values may change.
- Use const for variables with fixed values.

- Avoid using var in modern JavaScript.

1.2 Data Types

Primitive Data Types:

- **String:** Text data. Example: "Hello, world!"
- **Number:** Numeric data. Example: 42
- **Boolean:** Logical data (true or false).
- **Undefined:** A variable declared but not assigned a value.
- **Null:** Explicitly set to no value.

Example:

javascript

```
let name = "Alice";      // String
let age = 25;            // Number
let isStudent = true;    // Boolean
let hobby;               // Undefined
let favoriteBook = null;  // Null
```

Complex Data Types:

- **Object:** A collection of key-value pairs.
- **Array:** An ordered list of values.

javascript

```javascript
let user = { name: "Alice", age: 25 };  // Object
let colors = ["red", "green", "blue"]; // Array
```

1.3 Loops

Why Use Loops? Loops allow you to execute a block of code multiple times.

Types of Loops:

- **For Loop:**

  javascript

  ```javascript
  for (let i = 0; i < 5; i++) {
      console.log("Number:", i);
  }
  ```

- **While Loop:**

  javascript

  ```javascript
  let i = 0;
  while (i < 5) {
      console.log("Count:", i);
      i++;
  }
  ```

- **For...of Loop:**

  javascript

```
const fruits = ["apple", "banana", "cherry"];
for (const fruit of fruits) {
    console.log(fruit);
}
```

1.4 Functions

What are Functions? Functions are reusable blocks of code that perform a specific task.

Function Declaration:

javascript

```
function greet(name) {
    return `Hello, ${name}!`;
}
console.log(greet("Alice"));
```

Arrow Functions:

javascript

```
const add = (a, b) => a + b;
console.log(add(5, 3)); // Output: 8
```

2. DOM Manipulation

What is the DOM?

The DOM (Document Object Model) is a programming interface for web documents. It represents the structure of an HTML document and allows JavaScript to interact with elements.

2.1 Selecting Elements

Methods to Select Elements:

- **By ID:**

javascript

```
const title = document.getElementById("title");
```

- **By Class Name:**

javascript

```
const items = document.getElementsByClassName("item");
```

- **By Query Selector:**

javascript

```
const header = document.querySelector("header");
const buttons = document.querySelectorAll(".btn");
```

2.2 Modifying Elements

Changing Content:

javascript

```
const title = document.getElementById("title");
title.textContent = "Welcome to JavaScript!";
```

Changing Styles:

javascript

```
title.style.color = "blue";
title.style.fontSize = "24px";
```

Adding/Removing Classes:

javascript

```
title.classList.add("highlight");
title.classList.remove("highlight");
```

2.3 Creating and Removing Elements

Creating Elements:

javascript

```
const newItem = document.createElement("li");
newItem.textContent = "New List Item";
document.querySelector("ul").appendChild(newItem);
```

Removing Elements:

javascript

```
const item = document.querySelector(".item");
item.remove();
```

3. Event Handling

What are Events?

Events are user interactions or browser actions, such as clicks, key presses, or page loads.

3.1 Adding Event Listeners

Basic Event Listener:

javascript

```
const button = document.querySelector("button");
button.addEventListener("click", () => {
    alert("Button Clicked!");
});
```

Handling Multiple Events:

javascript

```
const input = document.querySelector("input");
input.addEventListener("focus", () => console.log("Input Focused"));
input.addEventListener("blur", () => console.log("Input Blurred"));
```

3.2 Event Object

Understanding the Event Object: The event object contains information about the event that occurred.

javascript

```javascript
document.addEventListener("click", (event) => {
    console.log("Clicked element:", event.target);
});
```

Preventing Default Behavior:

javascript

```javascript
const link = document.querySelector("a");
link.addEventListener("click", (event) => {
    event.preventDefault();
    console.log("Default link behavior prevented.");
});
```

---

4. Practical Example: Interactive To-Do List

HTML:

html

```html
<!DOCTYPE html>
<html lang="en">
<head>
    <meta charset="UTF-8">
    <meta name="viewport" content="width=device-width, initial-scale=1.0">
```

```
  <title>To-Do List</title>
</head>
<body>
  <h1>To-Do List</h1>
  <input type="text" id="taskInput" placeholder="Add a task">
  <button id="addTask">Add Task</button>
  <ul id="taskList"></ul>
  <script src="script.js"></script>
</body>
</html>
```

JavaScript:

javascript

```
const taskInput = document.getElementById("taskInput");
const addTaskButton = document.getElementById("addTask");
const taskList = document.getElementById("taskList");

// Add Task
addTaskButton.addEventListener("click", () => {
  const task = taskInput.value.trim();
  if (task) {
    const li = document.createElement("li");
    li.textContent = task;
    const removeButton = document.createElement("button");
    removeButton.textContent = "Remove";
    removeButton.addEventListener("click", () => li.remove());
    li.appendChild(removeButton);
    taskList.appendChild(li);
    taskInput.value = "";
  }
```

```
});
```

JavaScript is a powerful language for creating dynamic and interactive web pages. By mastering its core concepts, DOM manipulation, and event handling, you can build engaging, user-friendly applications. This foundational knowledge will prepare you for advanced JavaScript topics and frameworks in full stack development.

Chapter 6: Modern CSS Frameworks

Overview

CSS frameworks streamline the process of creating responsive and visually appealing web designs. Modern frameworks like Bootstrap, Tailwind CSS, and Material UI offer prebuilt styles, components, and utilities to help developers build professional-looking websites efficiently. This chapter introduces these frameworks and demonstrates how to use them for rapid layout development.

---

1. What Are CSS Frameworks?

Definition:

CSS frameworks are collections of prewritten CSS rules, components, and utilities that simplify and speed up the development of web layouts.

Why Use CSS Frameworks?

- **Efficiency:** Quickly build consistent designs with reusable styles.
- **Responsiveness:** Built-in grid systems and responsive utilities ensure designs adapt to all screen sizes.
- **Customization:** Frameworks can be tailored to specific project needs.

2. Introduction to Bootstrap

Overview:

Bootstrap is one of the most popular CSS frameworks, offering a robust grid system, predesigned components, and utilities.

Key Features:

- **Grid System:** A 12-column responsive grid.
- **Components:** Buttons, cards, modals, and more.
- **Utilities:** Classes for spacing, typography, colors, etc.

Getting Started:

1. **Include Bootstrap:** Use the Bootstrap CDN:

   html

   ```
   <link
   href="https://cdn.jsdelivr.net/npm/bootstrap@5.3.0/dist/css/bootstrap.min.css" rel="stylesheet">
   ```

2. **Example Layout:**

   html

   ```
   <div class="container">
     <div class="row">
   ```

```
            <div class="col-md-6">Left Column</div>
            <div class="col-md-6">Right Column</div>
        </div>
    </div>
```

Building a Responsive Navbar:

html

```
<nav class="navbar navbar-expand-lg navbar-light bg-light">
  <div class="container-fluid">
    <a class="navbar-brand" href="#">Brand</a>
    <button class="navbar-toggler" type="button" data-bs-toggle="collapse"
data-bs-target="#navbarNav">
      <span class="navbar-toggler-icon"></span>
    </button>
    <div class="collapse navbar-collapse" id="navbarNav">
      <ul class="navbar-nav">
        <li class="nav-item"><a class="nav-link" href="#">Home</a></li>
        <li class="nav-item"><a class="nav-link" href="#">Features</a></li>
        <li class="nav-item"><a class="nav-link" href="#">Pricing</a></li>
      </ul>
    </div>
  </div>
</nav>
```

3. Introduction to Tailwind CSS

Overview:

Tailwind CSS is a utility-first CSS framework that lets you design directly in your HTML with prebuilt utility classes.

Key Features:

- **Utility-First Approach:** Use classes for spacing, typography, colors, and more.
- **Customizable:** Fully customizable via configuration.
- **No Predefined Components:** Allows complete design flexibility.

Getting Started:

1. **Include Tailwind CSS:** Use the Tailwind CDN:

html

```html
<script src="https://cdn.tailwindcss.com"></script>
```

2. **Example Layout:**

html

```html
<div class="flex flex-col md:flex-row gap-4">
    <div class="w-full md:w-1/2 p-4 bg-gray-100">Left Column</div>
    <div class="w-full md:w-1/2 p-4 bg-gray-200">Right Column</div>
</div>
```

Building a Responsive Navbar:

html

```
<nav class="bg-blue-500 p-4">
  <div class="container mx-auto flex justify-between items-center">
    <a class="text-white text-xl font-bold" href="#">Brand</a>
    <ul class="hidden md:flex gap-4">
      <li><a class="text-white hover:underline" href="#">Home</a></li>
      <li><a class="text-white hover:underline" href="#">About</a></li>
      <li><a class="text-white hover:underline" href="#">Contact</a></li>
    </ul>
  </div>
</nav>
```

---

4. Introduction to Material UI

Overview:

Material UI (MUI) is a React-based UI framework that implements Google's Material Design principles.

Key Features:

- **React Components:** Prebuilt components for React applications.
- **Customizable:** Easily themed and styled.
- **Consistency:** Based on Material Design guidelines.

Getting Started:

1. **Install Material UI:**

bash

npm install @mui/material @emotion/react @emotion/styled

2. **Example Layout:**

javascript

```javascript
import React from 'react';
import { Container, Grid, Paper } from '@mui/material';

function App() {
  return (
    <Container>
      <Grid container spacing={2}>
        <Grid item xs={12} md={6}>
          <Paper style={{ padding: '16px' }}>Left Column</Paper>
        </Grid>
        <Grid item xs={12} md={6}>
          <Paper style={{ padding: '16px' }}>Right Column</Paper>
        </Grid>
      </Grid>
    </Container>
  );
}

export default App;
```

Building a Responsive Navbar:

javascript

```
import React from 'react';
import { AppBar, Toolbar, Typography, Button } from '@mui/material';

function Navbar() {
  return (
    <AppBar position="static">
      <Toolbar>
        <Typography variant="h6" style={{ flexGrow: 1 }}>
          Brand
        </Typography>
        <Button color="inherit">Home</Button>
        <Button color="inherit">About</Button>
        <Button color="inherit">Contact</Button>
      </Toolbar>
    </AppBar>
  );
}

export default Navbar;
```

---

5. Building Responsive Layouts with Frameworks

Responsive Design with Bootstrap:
Bootstrap's grid system makes building responsive layouts straightforward.

Example: Three-Column Layout

html

```
<div class="container">
  <div class="row">
    <div class="col-md-4">Column 1</div>
    <div class="col-md-4">Column 2</div>
    <div class="col-md-4">Column 3</div>
  </div>
</div>
```

Responsive Design with Tailwind CSS:

Tailwind CSS uses utility classes to create responsive designs.

Example: Two-Column Layout

html

```
<div class="grid grid-cols-1 md:grid-cols-2 gap-4">
  <div class="p-4 bg-blue-100">Column 1</div>
  <div class="p-4 bg-blue-200">Column 2</div>
</div>
```

Responsive Design with Material UI:

Material UI uses its Grid system for responsive layouts.

Example: Three-Column Layout

javascript

```
import React from 'react';
```

```
import { Grid, Paper } from '@mui/material';

function ResponsiveLayout() {
  return (
    <Grid container spacing={2}>
      <Grid item xs={12} sm={6} md={4}>
        <Paper>Column 1</Paper>
      </Grid>
      <Grid item xs={12} sm={6} md={4}>
        <Paper>Column 2</Paper>
      </Grid>
      <Grid item xs={12} sm={6} md={4}>
        <Paper>Column 3</Paper>
      </Grid>
    </Grid>
  );
}

export default ResponsiveLayout;
```

---

6. Choosing the Right Framework

Feature	Bootstrap	Tailwind CSS	Material UI
Ease of Use	Beginner-Friendly	Flexible, Requires Learning	Ideal for React Users

Feature	Bootstrap	Tailwind CSS	Material UI
Customization	Moderate	High	High
Prebuilt Components	Extensive	Minimal	Extensive
Responsiveness	Built-In Grid System	Utility Classes	Grid System

Modern CSS frameworks like Bootstrap, Tailwind CSS, and Material UI significantly reduce the time and effort needed to build responsive, visually appealing web layouts. By understanding their unique strengths and features, you can choose the right framework for your project and accelerate your front-end development workflow.

Chapter 6: Introduction to JavaScript Frameworks

Overview

JavaScript frameworks like React, Angular, and Vue.js simplify the development of dynamic, scalable, and efficient web applications. They provide structured tools, reusable components, and efficient data handling methods, enabling developers to build complex projects faster and with fewer errors. This chapter explores the importance of JavaScript frameworks, compares the most popular ones, and helps you choose the right framework for your project.

---

1. What Are JavaScript Frameworks?

Definition:

JavaScript frameworks are libraries or tools that provide a structured way to build interactive and responsive web applications. They abstract repetitive tasks, manage application state, and offer reusable UI components.

Key Features of Frameworks:

- **Component-Based Architecture:** Build reusable, modular UI elements.

- **Efficient State Management:** Manage and synchronize data across components.
- **Routing:** Enable navigation between views without reloading the page.
- **Tooling Ecosystem:** Integrate with build tools, testing libraries, and deployment pipelines.

2. Why Are Frameworks Essential?

2.1 Simplified Development Process

Frameworks provide prebuilt functionality for common tasks, such as DOM manipulation, event handling, and API calls, reducing boilerplate code.

2.2 Scalability

They help organize code into components or modules, making it easier to scale applications as they grow.

2.3 Reusability

Reusable components save time and effort when building or updating features.

2.4 Performance Optimization

Modern frameworks are optimized for speed, often including features like virtual DOM, lazy loading, and code splitting.

2.5 Community and Ecosystem

Popular frameworks come with extensive community support, documentation, and libraries to solve almost any development challenge.

---

3. Popular JavaScript Frameworks

3.1 React

Overview: React, developed by Facebook, is a library for building user interfaces with a focus on component-based development.

Key Features:

- **Virtual DOM:** Improves performance by minimizing direct DOM manipulation.
- **JSX Syntax:** Combines HTML and JavaScript for declarative coding.
- **Unidirectional Data Flow:** Ensures predictable state management.

Ideal For:

- Large-scale applications requiring dynamic updates.
- Projects requiring custom UI solutions.

Example:

javascript

```
import React from 'react';
import ReactDOM from 'react-dom';

function App() {
  return <h1>Hello, React!</h1>;
}

ReactDOM.render(<App />, document.getElementById('root'));
```

3.2 Angular

Overview: Angular, developed by Google, is a full-fledged framework for building robust, enterprise-grade applications.

Key Features:

- **Two-Way Data Binding:** Synchronizes data between the model and view.
- **Dependency Injection:** Simplifies component dependencies.
- **TypeScript-Based:** Enhances code quality with static typing.

Ideal For:

- Large-scale, enterprise-level applications.
- Complex, feature-rich projects with a need for built-in tools.

Example:

typescript

```
import { Component } from '@angular/core';

@Component({
  selector: 'app-root',
  template: '<h1>Hello, Angular!</h1>',
})
export class AppComponent {}
```

3.3 Vue.js

Overview: Vue.js is a lightweight and flexible framework that combines the best of React and Angular, offering an easy learning curve.

Key Features:

- **Reactivity System:** Automatically updates the DOM when data changes.
- **Component-Based:** Supports modular UI development.
- **Flexible Integration:** Works seamlessly with existing projects.

Ideal For:

- Small to medium-scale applications.

- Projects requiring easy integration with other libraries or frameworks.

Example:

javascript

import { createApp } from 'vue';

const App = {
  template: '<h1>Hello, Vue.js!</h1>',
};

createApp(App).mount('#app');

---

4. Comparing React, Angular, and Vue.js

Feature	React	Angular	Vue.js
Type	Library	Full Framework	Framework
Learning Curve	Moderate	Steep (TypeScript required)	Easy
Performance	High (Virtual DOM)	High (Optimized by Angular)	High (Virtual DOM)

Feature	React	Angular	Vue.js
State Management	External libraries (Redux)	Built-in	Vuex
Ideal For	Dynamic UI, large apps	Enterprise-grade applications	Flexible, smaller projects

5. Choosing the Right Framework

5.1 Consider Your Project's Scale

- **Small-Scale Projects:** Vue.js is lightweight and easy to set up.
- **Medium-Scale Projects:** React offers flexibility and scalability.
- **Large-Scale Projects:** Angular provides the structure and tools needed for complex applications.

5.2 Evaluate the Learning Curve

- If you're new to JavaScript frameworks, Vue.js has the easiest learning curve.
- For experienced developers, Angular's comprehensive ecosystem might be more appealing.

- React strikes a balance, requiring some learning but offering vast flexibility.

5.3 Integration Needs

- If you need to integrate into an existing project, React or Vue.js is a better fit due to their modular nature.
- Angular is best suited for standalone applications.

5.4 Community and Ecosystem

- **React:** Largest community and ecosystem.
- **Angular:** Extensive documentation and tools for enterprise needs.
- **Vue.js:** Rapidly growing with excellent community support.

---

6. Practical Example: Building a Simple Counter

React Implementation:

javascript

```
import React, { useState } from 'react';
import ReactDOM from 'react-dom';

function Counter() {
    const [count, setCount] = useState(0);
```

```
  return (
    <div>
      <h1>Count: {count}</h1>
      <button onClick={() => setCount(count + 1)}>Increment</button>
    </div>
  );
}


ReactDOM.render(<Counter />, document.getElementById('root'));
```

Angular Implementation:

typescript

```typescript
import { Component } from '@angular/core';


@Component({
  selector: 'app-counter',
  template: `
    <div>
      <h1>Count: {{ count }}</h1>
      <button (click)="increment()">Increment</button>
    </div>
  `,
})
export class CounterComponent {
  count = 0;

  increment() {
    this.count++;
```

```
    }
}
```

Vue.js Implementation:

javascript

```javascript
import { createApp } from 'vue';

const Counter = {
  data() {
    return { count: 0 };
  },
  template: `
    <div>
      <h1>Count: {{ count }}</h1>
      <button @click="count++">Increment</button>
    </div>
  `,
};

createApp(Counter).mount('#app');
```

JavaScript frameworks like React, Angular, and Vue.js are essential for building modern, scalable, and efficient web applications. Each framework has its strengths and is suited for specific use cases. By understanding their features and evaluating your project's needs, you can confidently choose the right framework to streamline your development process. In the following chapters, we'll dive deeper into these frameworks and their practical applications.

Chapter 8: Building with React

Overview

React is a popular JavaScript library for building dynamic and reusable user interfaces. This chapter focuses on React's key features, including components, state management, and lifecycle methods, along with modern concepts like hooks and functional components. By the end of this chapter, you'll understand how to create interactive web applications with React.

---

1. Components

What Are Components?

Components are the building blocks of a React application. Each component is a reusable and self-contained piece of UI.

Types of Components:

1. **Functional Components:** Written as functions, these are simpler and use React hooks for state and side effects.

   javascript

   ```javascript
   function Greeting() {
       return <h1>Hello, React!</h1>;
   }
   ```

2. **Class Components:** Written as ES6 classes, they include state and lifecycle methods.

javascript

```
class Greeting extends React.Component {
  render() {
    return <h1>Hello, React!</h1>;
  }
}
```

2. State Management

What Is State?

State is an object that represents the current data or UI of a component. It determines how the component behaves and renders.

Using State in Functional Components:

State can be managed in functional components using the useState hook.

javascript

```
import React, { useState } from 'react';

function Counter() {
  const [count, setCount] = useState(0);

  return (
```

```
    <div>
      <h1>Count: {count}</h1>
      <button onClick={() => setCount(count + 1)}>Increment</button>
    </div>
  );
}
```

State in Class Components:

State is defined in the constructor method and updated using this.setState.

javascript

```
class Counter extends React.Component {
  constructor() {
    super();
    this.state = { count: 0 };
  }

  increment = () => {
    this.setState({ count: this.state.count + 1 });
  };

  render() {
    return (
      <div>
        <h1>Count: {this.state.count}</h1>
        <button onClick={this.increment}>Increment</button>
      </div>
    );
  }
```

}

---

3. Lifecycle Methods

What Are Lifecycle Methods?
Lifecycle methods in class components allow you to perform actions at specific points in a component's life (e.g., when it mounts, updates, or unmounts).

Key Lifecycle Methods:

1. **componentDidMount:** Executes after the component is rendered.
2. **componentDidUpdate:** Executes after state or props change.
3. **componentWillUnmount:** Executes before the component is removed.

Example:

javascript

```
class Timer extends React.Component {
  componentDidMount() {
    console.log('Component mounted');
  }

  componentDidUpdate() {
    console.log('Component updated');
```

```
  }

  componentWillUnmount() {
    console.log('Component will unmount');
  }

  render() {
    return <h1>Timer</h1>;
  }
}
```

---

4. Hooks

What Are Hooks?

Hooks are functions introduced in React 16.8 that let you use state and other React features in functional components.

Common Hooks:

1. **useState:** Manages state in functional components.

   javascript

   ```
   const [count, setCount] = useState(0);
   ```

2. **useEffect:** Handles side effects like data fetching or DOM updates.

   javascript

```
useEffect(() => {
    console.log('Component rendered');
}, [count]); // Dependency array
```

3. **useContext:** Accesses context values without wrapping components in <Context.Provider>.

---

5. Functional Components

Advantages of Functional Components:

- Simpler and more readable.
- Hooks eliminate the need for lifecycle methods in many cases.
- Perform better than class components in terms of rendering.

Example: Fetching Data with useEffect:

javascript

```
import React, { useState, useEffect } from 'react';

function DataFetcher() {
  const [data, setData] = useState([]);

  useEffect(() => {
    fetch('https://jsonplaceholder.typicode.com/posts')
```

```javascript
      .then((response) => response.json())
      .then((data) => setData(data));
  }, []);

  return (
    <ul>
      {data.map((item) => (
        <li key={item.id}>{item.title}</li>
      ))}
    </ul>
  );
}
```

---

6. Building a Simple Application

Task: Create a Todo List App.

Step 1: Todo Component

javascript

```javascript
function TodoList() {
  const [tasks, setTasks] = useState([]);
  const [task, setTask] = useState("");

  const addTask = () => {
    if (task) {
      setTasks([...tasks, task]);
      setTask("");
    }
```

```
};

  return (
    <div>
      <input
        type="text"
        value={task}
        onChange={(e) => setTask(e.target.value)}
      />
      <button onClick={addTask}>Add Task</button>
      <ul>
        {tasks.map((task, index) => (
          <li key={index}>{task}</li>
        ))}
      </ul>
    </div>
  );
}
```

7. Summary

- **Components:** Fundamental building blocks of React apps.
- **State Management:** Manage dynamic data using useState or class-based state.
- **Lifecycle Methods:** Allow class components to perform specific actions at different stages.
- **Hooks:** Simplify state and side-effect management in functional components.

React simplifies the development of dynamic user interfaces with its component-based architecture and powerful features like hooks and lifecycle methods. By mastering these concepts, you can create scalable, maintainable, and efficient web applications. In the next chapter, we will explore advanced React topics, including routing and global state management with Redux.

Chapter 9: Advanced React Development

Overview

As React applications grow in complexity, advanced features like routing, global state management, and context-sharing become essential. This chapter delves into React Router for managing navigation, the Context API for passing data across components, and Redux for robust state management in large-scale applications.

---

1. Routing with React Router

1.1 What is React Router?

React Router is a library for managing navigation and routing in React applications. It enables users to navigate between different views without reloading the page.

1.2 Installing React Router

To add React Router to your project:

bash

npm install react-router-dom

1.3 Basic Routing

React Router uses components like BrowserRouter, Routes, and Route to define navigation paths.

Example: Setting Up Routes

javascript

```javascript
import React from 'react';
import { BrowserRouter as Router, Routes, Route } from 'react-router-dom';

function Home() {
  return <h1>Home Page</h1>;
}

function About() {
  return <h1>About Page</h1>;
}

function App() {
  return (
    <Router>
      <Routes>
        <Route path="/" element={<Home />} />
        <Route path="/about" element={<About />} />
      </Routes>
    </Router>
  );
}

export default App;
```

1.4 Navigation with Links

Replace traditional anchor tags with the Link component to enable SPA navigation.

Example:

javascript

```
import { Link } from 'react-router-dom';

function Navbar() {
  return (
    <nav>
      <Link to="/">Home</Link>
      <Link to="/about">About</Link>
    </nav>
  );
}
```

1.5 Dynamic Routing

Dynamic routes handle parameters in the URL using useParams.

Example:

javascript

```
import React from 'react';
import { useParams } from 'react-router-dom';

function Profile() {
  const { username } = useParams();
  return <h1>Welcome, {username}!</h1>;
```

```
}
```

```
// Route setup
<Route path="/profile/:username" element={<Profile />} />
```

---

2. State Management with Context API

2.1 What is the Context API?

The Context API allows data to be shared across components without passing props manually through every level of the component tree.

2.2 Creating a Context

Use React.createContext to define a context.

Example:

javascript

```javascript
import React, { createContext, useState } from 'react';

export const ThemeContext = createContext();

function ThemeProvider({ children }) {
  const [theme, setTheme] = useState('light');

  return (
    <ThemeContext.Provider value={{ theme, setTheme }}>
      {children}
```

```
    </ThemeContext.Provider>
  );
}
```

export default ThemeProvider;

2.3 Consuming Context

Access context data in child components using the useContext hook.

Example:

javascript

```
import React, { useContext } from 'react';
import { ThemeContext } from './ThemeProvider';

function ToggleTheme() {
  const { theme, setTheme } = useContext(ThemeContext);

  return (
    <button onClick={() => setTheme(theme === 'light' ? 'dark' : 'light')}>
      Switch to {theme === 'light' ? 'Dark' : 'Light'} Mode
    </button>
  );
}
```

2.4 Wrapping the Application

Wrap the application with the ThemeProvider to make context available globally.

javascript

```
import React from 'react';
import ThemeProvider from './ThemeProvider';
import App from './App';

function Root() {
  return (
    <ThemeProvider>
      <App />
    </ThemeProvider>
  );
}

export default Root;
```

---

3. State Management with Redux

3.1 What is Redux?

Redux is a predictable state management library that centralizes application state in a single store. It is ideal for large-scale applications with complex state interactions.

3.2 Installing Redux

Install Redux and React bindings:

bash

```
npm install redux react-redux
```

3.3 Key Concepts in Redux

- **Store:** Holds the application state.
- **Actions:** Describe what happened (e.g., increment a counter).
- **Reducers:** Define how state changes in response to actions.

3.4 Setting Up Redux

Step 1: Create an Action Actions are plain objects that describe changes to the state.

javascript

```javascript
export const increment = () => {
  return { type: 'INCREMENT' };
};
```

Step 2: Create a Reducer Reducers specify how the state is updated based on actions.

javascript

```javascript
const counterReducer = (state = 0, action) => {
  switch (action.type) {
    case 'INCREMENT':
      return state + 1;
    default:
      return state;
  }
};
```

export default counterReducer;

Step 3: Create a Store The store holds the global state.

javascript

```
import { createStore } from 'redux';
import counterReducer from './reducers';

const store = createStore(counterReducer);
export default store;
```

Step 4: Provide the Store Wrap your application with the Provider component to make the store accessible.

javascript

```
import React from 'react';
import { Provider } from 'react-redux';
import store from './store';
import App from './App';

function Root() {
  return (
    <Provider store={store}>
      <App />
    </Provider>
  );
}

export default Root;
```

Step 5: Access State in Components Use the useSelector and useDispatch hooks to interact with the store.

javascript

```
import React from 'react';
import { useSelector, useDispatch } from 'react-redux';
import { increment } from './actions';

function Counter() {
  const count = useSelector((state) => state);
  const dispatch = useDispatch();

  return (
    <div>
      <h1>Count: {count}</h1>
      <button onClick={() => dispatch(increment())}>Increment</button>
    </div>
  );
}
```

4. Comparing Context API and Redux

Feature	Context API	Redux
Use Case	Small to medium-sized applications	Large-scale, complex applications

Feature	Context API	Redux
Ease of Use	Easy to set up	Steeper learning curve
Performance	Slower for deeply nested trees	Optimized for large applications
Tooling	Minimal	Extensive dev tools available

---

5. Building an Application with React Router and Redux

Task: Create a shopping cart application.

1. **Use React Router** to navigate between pages (e.g., products and cart).
2. **Use Redux** to manage the cart state globally.
3. **Combine Components** to create a seamless shopping experience.

Key Features:

- Add items to the cart.
- View and remove items from the cart.
- Navigate between product listings and the cart.

Advanced React development techniques like routing with React Router and state management using Context API or Redux enable developers to build scalable and maintainable applications. These tools provide robust solutions for handling complex data flows and navigation, essential for modern web applications. The next chapter will explore Vue.js, another powerful framework for building user interfaces.

Chapter 10: Building User Interfaces with Vue.js

Overview

Vue.js is a progressive JavaScript framework designed to simplify the process of building user interfaces. It offers a powerful yet easy-to-learn structure for managing components, handling events, and using directives. This chapter introduces Vue.js fundamentals, including components, directives, event handling, and advanced features like Vuex for state management and Vue Router for navigation.

---

1. Getting Started with Vue.js

1.1 What is Vue.js?

Vue.js is a flexible and approachable JavaScript framework for building dynamic user interfaces. It supports incremental adoption, meaning you can use it for small projects or scale it up for complex single-page applications (SPAs).

1.2 Installing Vue.js

1. **Using CDN:**

   html

```
<script src="https://cdn.jsdelivr.net/npm/vue@3"></script>
```

2. **Using npm:**

   bash

   npm install vue

3. **Creating a New Project with Vue CLI:**

   bash

   npm install -g @vue/cli
   vue create my-vue-app
   cd my-vue-app
   npm run serve

---

2. Components in Vue.js

2.1 What Are Components?

Components are reusable and self-contained pieces of UI, making it easier to build modular and scalable applications.

2.2 Defining a Component

javascript

```
// In a Single File Component (SFC)
<template>
```

```
  <div>
    <h1>Hello, {{ name }}!</h1>
    <button @click="changeName">Change Name</button>
  </div>
</template>

<script>
export default {
  data() {
    return {
      name: "Vue.js",
    };
  },
  methods: {
    changeName() {
      this.name = "World";
    },
  },
};
</script>

<style>
h1 {
  color: blue;
}
</style>
```

2.3 Using Components

Register components locally or globally.

Local Registration:

javascript

```
import HelloWorld from './HelloWorld.vue';

export default {
 components: {
  HelloWorld,
 },
};
```

Global Registration:

javascript

```
import { createApp } from 'vue';
import HelloWorld from './HelloWorld.vue';

const app = createApp(App);
app.component('HelloWorld', HelloWorld);
app.mount('#app');
```

---

3. Directives in Vue.js

3.1 What Are Directives?

Directives are special tokens in Vue templates that bind DOM elements to JavaScript logic.

Common Directives:

1. **v-bind:** Binds attributes or properties to expressions.

html

```
<img v-bind:src="imageUrl" />
```

2. **v-model:** Creates two-way binding between form inputs and data.

html

```
<input v-model="name" />
```

3. **v-for:** Renders a list of items.

html

```
<ul>
  <li v-for="item in items" :key="item.id">{{ item.name }}</li>
</ul>
```

4. **v-if / v-else-if / v-else:** Conditionally render elements.

html

```
<p v-if="isVisible">Visible</p>
<p v-else>Not Visible</p>
```

---

4. Event Handling in Vue.js

4.1 Listening to Events

Use the v-on directive or the shorthand @ to handle events.

Example:

html

```
<button @click="handleClick">Click Me</button>
```

Methods:

javascript

```
export default {
  methods: {
    handleClick() {
      alert("Button Clicked!");
    },
  },
};
```

4.2 Event Modifiers

- **@click.prevent:** Prevents the default action.
- **@click.stop:** Stops event propagation.
- **Example:**

  html

  ```
  <form @submit.prevent="submitForm">
    <button type="submit">Submit</button>
  </form>
  ```

5. State Management with Vuex

5.1 What is Vuex?

Vuex is a state management library for Vue.js applications. It centralizes application state and ensures predictable state updates.

5.2 Installing Vuex

bash

npm install vuex

5.3 Setting Up Vuex

1. **Create a Store:**

   javascript

   ```javascript
   import { createStore } from 'vuex';

   const store = createStore({
     state() {
      return {
        count: 0,
      };
     },
     mutations: {
      increment(state) {
        state.count++;
      },
     },
   ```

```
actions: {
  incrementAsync({ commit }) {
    setTimeout(() => {
      commit('increment');
    }, 1000);
  },
},
});
```

```
export default store;
```

2. **Use the Store:** Wrap your app with the store:

javascript

```javascript
import { createApp } from 'vue';
import App from './App.vue';
import store from './store';


createApp(App).use(store).mount('#app');
```

3. **Access State and Mutations:**

javascript

```javascript
import { useStore } from 'vuex';

export default {
  setup() {
    const store = useStore();
```

```
return {
  count: store.state.count,
  increment: () => store.commit('increment'),
};
},
};
```

6. Navigation with Vue Router

6.1 What is Vue Router?

Vue Router is the official router for Vue.js applications, enabling navigation between views in a single-page application.

6.2 Installing Vue Router

bash

```
npm install vue-router
```

6.3 Setting Up Vue Router

1. **Create Routes:**

javascript

```
import { createRouter, createWebHistory } from 'vue-router';
import Home from './views/Home.vue';
import About from './views/About.vue';

const routes = [
```

```
  { path: '/', component: Home },
  { path: '/about', component: About },
];

const router = createRouter({
  history: createWebHistory(),
  routes,
});

export default router;
```

2. Use the Router:

javascript

```
import { createApp } from 'vue';
import App from './App.vue';
import router from './router';

createApp(App).use(router).mount('#app');
```

3. Add Navigation Links:

html

```
<nav>
  <router-link to="/">Home</router-link>
  <router-link to="/about">About</router-link>
</nav>
```

7. Building a Simple Application

Task: To-Do List with Vuex and Vue Router

1. **Home Page:** Display tasks from Vuex state.
2. **Add Task Page:** Add tasks to Vuex state.

Key Features:

- Vue Router for navigation between pages.
- Vuex for state management of tasks.

Vue.js simplifies the process of building dynamic, modular, and scalable user interfaces. Its intuitive components, powerful directives, and advanced features like Vuex and Vue Router make it a versatile choice for web development. Mastering these tools will enable you to create efficient and maintainable applications. The next chapter will delve into back-end development essentials with Node.js.

Chapter 11: Introduction to Server-Side Development

Overview

The back-end is the backbone of any web application, handling data processing, storage, and business logic. This chapter explores the critical role of back-end development, introduces client-server architecture, and lays the foundation for building robust server-side applications.

---

1. What is Back-End Development?

Definition:

Back-end development involves creating the server-side logic and infrastructure that power web applications. It focuses on:

- **Data Processing:** Handling and transforming user data.
- **Database Operations:** Storing, retrieving, and managing data.
- **APIs:** Facilitating communication between the front-end and the server.

Why is Back-End Important?

- Ensures secure and efficient data handling.

- Manages application logic and workflows.
- Facilitates integration with third-party services (e.g., payment gateways, external APIs).

---

2. The Role of Back-End in Web Applications

2.1 Managing Business Logic

The back-end implements the core functionality of an application. For example:

- Authenticating users.
- Calculating and storing financial transactions.
- Processing orders in an e-commerce site.

2.2 Database Operations

Back-end applications interact with databases to:

- Save user data (e.g., user profiles, transactions).
- Retrieve and send data to the front-end for display.

2.3 Security

The back-end ensures data security by:

- Encrypting sensitive information (e.g., passwords, payment data).
- Implementing access controls and validating user input.

2.4 Communication with the Front-End

The back-end serves as the middle layer between the user interface (front-end) and the database. It processes client requests, interacts with the database, and sends appropriate responses back to the front-end.

---

3. Understanding Client-Server Architecture

3.1 What is Client-Server Architecture?

Client-server architecture is a model where the client (browser or mobile app) requests data or services from a server. The server processes these requests and responds with the required data or actions.

3.2 Key Components:

Component Description

Client	The front-end or user interface of the application. Sends requests to the server (e.g., web browsers).
Server	The back-end logic that processes requests and manages data.

Component Description

Database	Stores application data that the server retrieves or modifies.
API	A set of endpoints the client uses to interact with the server.

3.3 How Client-Server Communication Works:

1. **Client Request:** The user interacts with the application (e.g., submits a form).
   - Example: A user searches for "laptops" on an e-commerce website.
2. **Server Processing:** The server processes the request, retrieves data from the database, and prepares a response.
3. **Server Response:** The server sends the response back to the client.
   - Example: The server returns a list of laptops to the front-end for display.

4. Protocols and Tools for Communication

4.1 HTTP/HTTPS:

- **HTTP (Hypertext Transfer Protocol):** The foundation of data communication on the web.
- **HTTPS:** A secure version of HTTP using encryption (SSL/TLS).

4.2 RESTful APIs:

- REST (Representational State Transfer) APIs define a set of rules for building scalable and stateless interactions between the client and server.
- **Example:** A REST API endpoint to fetch products:

http

GET /api/products

4.3 WebSockets:

- WebSockets enable real-time, bidirectional communication between the client and server.
- **Example Use Case:** Chat applications.

---

5. Server-Side Languages and Frameworks

Popular Back-End Languages:

Language Strengths

Node.js	JavaScript runtime for building fast, scalable applications.
Python	Versatile and beginner-friendly, with frameworks like Django and Flask.
Java	Robust and widely used for enterprise-level applications.
Ruby	Simplifies web development with the Rails framework.
PHP	Commonly used for server-side scripting and CMS platforms like WordPress.

Why Choose Node.js?

- Uses JavaScript for both front-end and back-end, reducing context switching.
- Supports asynchronous programming for handling multiple requests efficiently.
- Large ecosystem with npm (Node Package Manager).

6. Practical Example: Building a Simple HTTP Server with Node.js

Step 1: Install Node.js

Download and install Node.js from Node.js Official Website.

Step 2: Create a Basic Server

javascript

```javascript
// Import the http module
const http = require('http');

// Create a server
const server = http.createServer((req, res) => {
  if (req.url === '/') {
    res.writeHead(200, { 'Content-Type': 'text/plain' });
    res.end('Welcome to the Back-End!');
  } else if (req.url === '/about') {
    res.writeHead(200, { 'Content-Type': 'text/plain' });
    res.end('This is the About Page');
  } else {
    res.writeHead(404, { 'Content-Type': 'text/plain' });
    res.end('Page Not Found');
  }
});

// Start the server
server.listen(3000, () => {
  console.log('Server running on http://localhost:3000');
});
```

7. Tools for Back-End Development

Tool	Purpose
Postman	Testing and debugging APIs.
Docker	Containerizing back-end applications.
MongoDB Compass	Visualizing and managing MongoDB databases.
PM2	Managing and monitoring Node.js applications.

8. Real-World Use Cases of Back-End Development

1. **E-Commerce Platforms:**
   o Manage inventory, process orders, and handle payments securely.
2. **Social Media Applications:**
   o Handle user authentication, data sharing, and real-time updates.
3. **Content Management Systems (CMS):**
   o Enable users to create, edit, and publish content dynamically.
4. **Data-Driven Dashboards:**
   o Aggregate and process data for analytics.

9. Best Practices for Back-End Development

1. **Follow Security Principles:**
   - Use HTTPS.
   - Validate and sanitize user inputs.
   - Encrypt sensitive data.
2. **Optimize Performance:**
   - Use caching (e.g., Redis) to reduce database load.
   - Optimize database queries.
3. **Write Scalable Code:**
   - Structure code into reusable modules.
   - Use load balancers for handling increased traffic.
4. **Implement Logging:**
   - Use logging tools (e.g., Winston, Bunyan) to track errors and monitor performance.

The back-end is the powerhouse of a web application, providing the infrastructure for data management, logic, and security. Understanding its role and the client-server architecture is essential for building scalable and efficient web applications. In the next chapter, we'll explore Node.js fundamentals and how to leverage it for building powerful server-side applications.

Chapter 12: Node.js Fundamentals

Overview

Node.js is a runtime environment that allows developers to execute JavaScript on the server side. Known for its event-driven architecture and support for asynchronous programming, Node.js enables the creation of scalable, high-performance web applications. This chapter covers the fundamentals of Node.js, including its architecture and asynchronous nature, along with a hands-on example of building a simple server.

---

1. What is Node.js?

Definition:

Node.js is a JavaScript runtime built on Chrome's V8 engine. It enables developers to use JavaScript to build server-side applications.

Key Features:

- **Event-Driven Architecture:** Handles multiple requests efficiently through events and callbacks.
- **Non-Blocking I/O:** Supports asynchronous operations, preventing blocking of the main thread.

- **Scalability:** Ideal for applications requiring high concurrency, such as chat applications and real-time data services.
- **npm (Node Package Manager):** Provides access to a vast library of reusable packages.

Why Use Node.js?

- Uses a single programming language (JavaScript) for both front-end and back-end.
- Offers fast execution and lightweight resource usage.
- Supported by a large, active community.

2. Event-Driven Architecture

What is Event-Driven Architecture?

In Node.js, operations are triggered by events. Instead of waiting for a task to complete, Node.js uses an **event loop** to handle multiple requests asynchronously.

How It Works:

1. The server receives a request.
2. Node.js processes the request asynchronously (e.g., accessing a database).

3. Once the operation is complete, a callback function handles the result.

Example: Event-Driven Programming

javascript

```javascript
const EventEmitter = require('events');

// Create an event emitter
const emitter = new EventEmitter();

// Register an event listener
emitter.on('greet', (name) => {
  console.log(`Hello, ${name}!`);
});

// Trigger the event
emitter.emit('greet', 'Alice');
```

---

3. Asynchronous Programming

What is Asynchronous Programming?

Asynchronous programming allows tasks to run in parallel, enabling other operations to continue while waiting for long-running processes to complete.

Callback Functions:

A callback function is passed as an argument to another function and executes after the completion of a task.

javascript

```javascript
setTimeout(() => {
  console.log('This message is delayed by 2 seconds.');
}, 2000);

console.log('This message is shown immediately.');
```

Promises:

Promises represent the eventual completion or failure of an asynchronous operation.

javascript

```javascript
const fetchData = () => {
  return new Promise((resolve, reject) => {
    setTimeout(() => resolve('Data fetched!'), 1000);
  });
};

fetchData().then((message) => console.log(message));
```

Async/Await:

async and await provide a cleaner syntax for handling asynchronous code.

javascript

```
const fetchData = async () => {
    const data = await new Promise((resolve) => {
        setTimeout(() => resolve('Data fetched!'), 1000);
    });
    console.log(data);
};


fetchData();
```

---

4. Setting Up Node.js

Step 1: Install Node.js

1. Download and install Node.js from the official website.
2. Verify installation:

    bash

    node --version
    npm --version

Step 2: Initialize a Project

Create a project directory and initialize it:

bash

mkdir my-node-app
cd my-node-app
npm init -y

5. Building a Simple Server with Node.js

5.1 Import the *http* Module

The http module allows you to create an HTTP server.

5.2 Create a Server

javascript

```javascript
const http = require('http');

// Create a server
const server = http.createServer((req, res) => {
    // Set the response header
    res.writeHead(200, { 'Content-Type': 'text/plain' });

    // Respond based on the URL
    if (req.url === '/') {
        res.end('Welcome to the Home Page!');
    } else if (req.url === '/about') {
        res.end('About Us: Node.js Fundamentals');
    } else {
        res.writeHead(404);
        res.end('Page Not Found');
    }
});

// Start the server
server.listen(3000, () => {
```

```
console.log('Server is running on http://localhost:3000');
});
```

5.3 Run the Server

Save the file (e.g., server.js) and run it:

bash

node server.js

Visit http://localhost:3000 in your browser to see the output.

---

6. Handling Asynchronous Operations in Node.js

Example: Reading a File Asynchronously

Use the fs (File System) module to handle file operations.

javascript

```javascript
const fs = require('fs');

// Read a file asynchronously
fs.readFile('example.txt', 'utf8', (err, data) => {
    if (err) {
        console.error('Error reading file:', err);
    } else {
        console.log('File content:', data);
    }
});
```

Example: Writing to a File Asynchronously

javascript

```javascript
fs.writeFile('example.txt', 'Hello, Node.js!', (err) => {
  if (err) {
    console.error('Error writing to file:', err);
  } else {
    console.log('File written successfully.');
  }
});
```

7. Best Practices in Node.js Development

1. **Use Asynchronous Methods:** Prefer non-blocking (async) methods to maintain performance.

2. **Handle Errors Gracefully:** Always handle errors using try-catch or callbacks.

3. **Organize Code:** Split functionality into modules for better maintainability.

4. **Use Environment Variables:** Store sensitive data like API keys in .env files.

8. Real-World Use Cases of Node.js

1. **Real-Time Applications:**

o   Chat applications.

o   Live dashboards.

2. **RESTful APIs:**

o   Data-driven web applications.

o   Mobile app back-ends.

3. **Streaming Services:**

o   Video or audio streaming.

4. **IoT Applications:**

o   Handling high volumes of concurrent device connections.

Node.js revolutionizes server-side development by enabling developers to build scalable and high-performance applications using JavaScript. Its event-driven architecture and asynchronous programming model make it a versatile choice for real-time and data-intensive applications. In the next chapter, we will explore Express.js, a framework that simplifies Node.js application development.

Chapter 13: Express.js for Web Development

Overview

Express.js is a fast, minimalist web application framework for Node.js. It simplifies the process of building web applications and APIs by providing powerful tools for routing, middleware, and HTTP request handling. This chapter introduces the basics of setting up an Express.js application, defining routes, using middleware, and creating RESTful APIs.

---

1. What is Express.js?

Definition:

Express.js is a framework built on top of Node.js that simplifies server-side development. It provides abstractions and utilities for routing, middleware, and HTTP methods.

Key Features:

- **Routing:** Define endpoints to handle various HTTP requests.
- **Middleware:** Process requests before sending responses.
- **Templating:** Render dynamic HTML with template engines like EJS or Handlebars.
- **API Creation:** Build RESTful APIs efficiently.

2. Setting Up Express.js

Step 1: Install Express.js

1. Ensure Node.js is installed.
2. Create a new project and install Express:

bash

```
mkdir express-app
cd express-app
npm init -y
npm install express
```

Step 2: Create a Basic Server

Create a file named app.js:

javascript

```
const express = require('express');
const app = express();

// Define a route
app.get('/', (req, res) => {
    res.send('Welcome to Express.js!');
});

// Start the server
const PORT = 3000;
```

```
app.listen(PORT, () => {
    console.log(`Server is running on http://localhost:${PORT}`);
});
```

Run the server:

bash

node app.js

---

3. Defining Routes

What Are Routes?

Routes define how your application responds to client requests for specific URLs.

Route Methods:

- **GET:** Retrieve data.
- **POST:** Submit data to the server.
- **PUT:** Update existing data.
- **DELETE:** Remove data.

Example: Defining Routes

javascript

```
app.get('/about', (req, res) => {
    res.send('About Page');
});
```

```javascript
app.post('/submit', (req, res) => {
  res.send('Form submitted!');
});


app.put('/update', (req, res) => {
  res.send('Resource updated!');
});


app.delete('/delete', (req, res) => {
  res.send('Resource deleted!');
});
```

4. Middleware

What is Middleware?

Middleware functions are executed in the request-response cycle. They can:

- Process request data.
- Log requests.
- Handle authentication.
- Terminate requests.

Using Middleware:

- Apply middleware globally:

  javascript

```javascript
app.use((req, res, next) => {
    console.log(`${req.method} request for ${req.url}`);
    next();
});
```

- Apply middleware to specific routes:

javascript

```javascript
const logger = (req, res, next) => {
    console.log('Middleware applied to this route');
    next();
};

app.get('/protected', logger, (req, res) => {
    res.send('Protected route');
});
```

Built-In Middleware:

1. **express.json():** Parses incoming JSON requests.

   javascript

   ```javascript
   app.use(express.json());
   ```

2. **express.urlencoded():** Parses URL-encoded data.

   javascript

```javascript
app.use(express.urlencoded({ extended: true }));
```

3. **express.static():** Serves static files.

javascript

```javascript
app.use(express.static('public'));
```

---

5. RESTful APIs

What Are RESTful APIs?

RESTful APIs follow a standard architecture for creating scalable, stateless, and maintainable APIs. They use HTTP methods to perform CRUD operations.

Defining RESTful Endpoints
Example: Simple CRUD API

javascript

```javascript
const express = require('express');
const app = express();

let items = [
    { id: 1, name: 'Item 1' },
    { id: 2, name: 'Item 2' },
```

```
];

// Middleware to parse JSON
app.use(express.json());

// GET all items
app.get('/api/items', (req, res) => {
  res.json(items);
});

// GET a single item by ID
app.get('/api/items/:id', (req, res) => {
  const item = items.find(i => i.id === parseInt(req.params.id));
  if (!item) return res.status(404).send('Item not found');
  res.json(item);
});

// POST a new item
app.post('/api/items', (req, res) => {
  const newItem = {
    id: items.length + 1,
    name: req.body.name,
  };
  items.push(newItem);
  res.status(201).json(newItem);
});

// PUT to update an item
app.put('/api/items/:id', (req, res) => {
  const item = items.find(i => i.id === parseInt(req.params.id));
```

```
    if (!item) return res.status(404).send('Item not found');
    item.name = req.body.name;
    res.json(item);
});


// DELETE an item
app.delete('/api/items/:id', (req, res) => {
    const index = items.findIndex(i => i.id === parseInt(req.params.id));
    if (index === -1) return res.status(404).send('Item not found');
    const deletedItem = items.splice(index, 1);
    res.json(deletedItem);
});


// Start the server
const PORT = 3000;
app.listen(PORT, () => {
    console.log(`Server running on http://localhost:${PORT}`);
});
```

---

6. Request and Response Objects

Request (req) Object:

Contains details about the client's request, such as:

- **Parameters:** req.params
- **Query Strings:** req.query
- **Body Data:** req.body

Response (res) Object:

Used to send data back to the client, such as:

- **HTML or Text:** res.send()
- **JSON:** res.json()
- **Status Codes:** res.status()

Example: Using Request and Response:

javascript

```
app.get('/greet/:name', (req, res) => {
    const name = req.params.name;
    res.status(200).send(`Hello, ${name}!`);
});
```

---

7. Error Handling in Express.js

Using Middleware for Error Handling:
Define a global error-handling middleware:

javascript

```
app.use((err, req, res, next) => {
    console.error(err.message);
    res.status(500).send('Internal Server Error');
});
```

Catching Errors in Routes:
Use try-catch for error-prone logic:

javascript

```javascript
app.get('/error', (req, res, next) => {
  try {
    throw new Error('Something went wrong!');
  } catch (err) {
    next(err);
  }
});
```

8. Best Practices for Express.js Development

1. **Use Middleware Wisely:** Optimize middleware placement to avoid unnecessary processing.
2. **Validate Inputs:** Use libraries like Joi or express-validator to validate incoming data.
3. **Secure Your Application:**
    - Use helmet for securing HTTP headers.
    - Implement rate-limiting to prevent abuse.
4. **Organize Routes:** Split routes into separate modules for better maintainability.

Express.js simplifies the process of building server-side applications with its intuitive routing, middleware, and request-handling features. By mastering these concepts, you can efficiently create scalable RESTful APIs and web applications. The next chapter will cover database basics, integrating your Express.js application with databases like MongoDB and MySQL.

Chapter 14: Database Basics

Overview

Databases are at the core of web applications, storing and managing the data required for functionality and user interactions. This chapter introduces the fundamental concepts of relational and NoSQL databases, highlights the differences between them, and covers the basics of SQL and data modeling.

---

1. What is a Database?

Definition:

A database is an organized collection of data that can be easily accessed, managed, and updated.

Types of Databases:

1. **Relational Databases (RDBMS):**
   - Use structured tables with rows and columns.
   - Data is organized based on predefined schemas.
   - Use SQL (Structured Query Language) for querying and managing data.
   - Examples: MySQL, PostgreSQL, Oracle Database.
2. **NoSQL Databases:**
   - Designed for flexibility and scalability.

- o Use unstructured or semi-structured data formats like JSON or BSON.

- o Suitable for hierarchical and non-relational data models.

- o Examples: MongoDB, Couchbase, Cassandra.

2. Relational vs. NoSQL Databases

Feature	Relational (RDBMS)	NoSQL
Data Structure	Tabular (rows and columns).	Key-value, document, graph, or columnar.
Schema	Predefined and rigid.	Dynamic and flexible.
Scalability	Vertical (scale-up).	Horizontal (scale-out).
Query Language	SQL.	Varies; often no standardized query language.
Use Case	Complex relationships and structured data.	Big data, real-time analytics, and hierarchical data.

3. Introduction to Relational Databases

Key Concepts:

1. **Tables:** Store data in rows and columns.
2. **Primary Key:** A unique identifier for each record.
3. **Foreign Key:** Links tables to establish relationships.
4. **Normalization:** Organizing data to reduce redundancy.

Example:

A simple database for a school might have these tables:

- **Students:**

StudentID	Name	Age	Grade
1	Alice	15	10
2	Bob	14	9

- **Courses:**

CourseID	Name	Instructor
101	Math	Dr. Smith
102	Science	Dr. Brown

- **Enrollments:**

  StudentID CourseID

StudentID	CourseID
1	101
2	102

---

4. Introduction to NoSQL Databases

Key Concepts:

1. **Document-Based Storage:** Data is stored as documents in formats like JSON or BSON.
2. **Collections:** Equivalent to tables in RDBMS, collections group similar documents.

Example in MongoDB:

json

```
{
  "StudentID": 1,
  "Name": "Alice",
  "Age": 15,
  "Courses": [
    { "CourseID": 101, "Name": "Math" },
    { "CourseID": 102, "Name": "Science" }
  ]
```

}

---

5. Introduction to SQL

What is SQL?

SQL (Structured Query Language) is a standard language for querying and managing data in relational databases.

Basic SQL Operations:

1. **Creating a Table:**

   sql

   ```
   CREATE TABLE Students (
       StudentID INT PRIMARY KEY,
       Name VARCHAR(50),
       Age INT,
       Grade INT
   );
   ```

2. **Inserting Data:**

   sql

   ```
   INSERT INTO Students (StudentID, Name, Age, Grade)
   VALUES (1, 'Alice', 15, 10);
   ```

3. **Retrieving Data:**

sql

```
SELECT * FROM Students;
```

4. **Updating Data:**

sql

```
UPDATE Students
SET Age = 16
WHERE StudentID = 1;
```

5. **Deleting Data:**

sql

```
DELETE FROM Students
WHERE StudentID = 1;
```

---

6. NoSQL Query Example (MongoDB)

Basic Operations:

1. **Inserting Data:**

javascript

```
db.students.insertOne({
    StudentID: 1,
    Name: "Alice",
```

```
        Age: 15,
        Grade: 10
});
```

2. Retrieving Data:

javascript

db.students.find();

3. Updating Data:

javascript

```
db.students.updateOne(
    { StudentID: 1 },
    { $set: { Age: 16 } }
);
```

4. Deleting Data:

javascript

db.students.deleteOne({ StudentID: 1 });

---

7. Data Modeling

What is Data Modeling?

Data modeling involves designing a structure for your database to meet the requirements of your application.

Steps in Data Modeling:

1. **Identify Entities:**
   - Determine the objects or concepts to store in the database (e.g., Students, Courses).
2. **Define Attributes:**
   - Identify properties of each entity (e.g., Name, Age, Grade).
3. **Establish Relationships:**
   - Determine how entities are connected (e.g., Students enroll in Courses).
4. **Normalize Data (For RDBMS):**
   - Minimize redundancy by organizing data into related tables.

Example: E-Commerce Application

- **Entities:**
  - Users, Products, Orders.
- **Attributes:**
  - Users: UserID, Name, Email.
  - Products: ProductID, Name, Price.
  - Orders: OrderID, UserID, ProductID, Quantity.

8. Choosing Between Relational and NoSQL Databases

When to Use Relational Databases:

- Applications with complex relationships (e.g., banking, ERP systems).
- Scenarios requiring data consistency and integrity.

When to Use NoSQL Databases:

- Applications with large-scale, unstructured data (e.g., social media, IoT).
- Real-time analytics or high-throughput scenarios.

9. Tools for Database Management

Tool	Purpose
MySQL Workbench	GUI for designing and managing MySQL databases.
pgAdmin	GUI for PostgreSQL databases.

Tool	Purpose
MongoDB Compass	GUI for visualizing MongoDB data.
DBeaver	Universal database management tool.

Understanding database basics is crucial for developing applications that efficiently handle and store data. Relational databases like MySQL and PostgreSQL provide robust solutions for structured data, while NoSQL databases like MongoDB offer flexibility for unstructured or hierarchical data. Mastering SQL and data modeling will equip you to design and implement databases that meet diverse application needs. In the next chapter, we will explore integrating databases with Express.js to create dynamic, data-driven web applications.

Chapter 15: Integrating MongoDB with Node.js

Overview

MongoDB is a popular NoSQL database designed for scalability and flexibility, and it integrates seamlessly with Node.js. Mongoose, a powerful ODM (Object Data Modeling) library, simplifies the process of working with MongoDB by providing tools for schema design, validation, and query building. This chapter covers the basics of integrating MongoDB with Node.js, performing CRUD operations, and designing schemas and relationships.

---

1. Setting Up MongoDB with Node.js

1.1 Installing MongoDB

1. Download and install MongoDB from the official website.
2. Start the MongoDB server:

bash

mongod

1.2 Installing Mongoose

Install Mongoose in your Node.js project:

bash

npm install mongoose

1.3 Connecting to MongoDB

Create a connection to your MongoDB database using Mongoose:

javascript

```javascript
const mongoose = require('mongoose');

// Connect to MongoDB
mongoose.connect('mongodb://localhost:27017/myDatabase', {
    useNewUrlParser: true,
    useUnifiedTopology: true,
});

const db = mongoose.connection;
db.on('error', console.error.bind(console, 'connection error:'));
db.once('open', () => {
    console.log('Connected to MongoDB!');
});
```

---

2. Designing Schemas in MongoDB

2.1 What is a Schema?

A schema defines the structure of documents in a MongoDB collection, including fields, data types, and validations.

Defining a Schema with Mongoose:

javascript

```javascript
const mongoose = require('mongoose');

const userSchema = new mongoose.Schema({
    name: { type: String, required: true },
    email: { type: String, required: true, unique: true },
    age: { type: Number, min: 0 },
    createdAt: { type: Date, default: Date.now },
});

const User = mongoose.model('User', userSchema);
```

---

3. CRUD Operations Using Mongoose

3.1 Create Documents

Use the .save() method or Model.create() to insert new documents.

Example:

javascript

```javascript
const newUser = new User({
    name: 'Alice',
    email: 'alice@example.com',
    age: 25,
});
```

```javascript
newUser.save()
  .then(user => console.log('User created:', user))
  .catch(err => console.error(err));
```

Or:

javascript

```javascript
User.create({ name: 'Bob', email: 'bob@example.com', age: 30 })
  .then(user => console.log('User created:', user))
  .catch(err => console.error(err));
```

3.2 Read Documents

Use .find() or .findOne() to retrieve data.

Example: Get All Users:

javascript

```javascript
User.find()
  .then(users => console.log('Users:', users))
  .catch(err => console.error(err));
```

Example: Get a Single User by Email:

javascript

```javascript
User.findOne({ email: 'alice@example.com' })
  .then(user => console.log('User found:', user))
  .catch(err => console.error(err));
```

3.3 Update Documents

Use .updateOne() or .findByIdAndUpdate() to modify existing documents.

Example: Update User's Age:

javascript

```javascript
User.updateOne({ email: 'alice@example.com' }, { age: 26 })
   .then(result => console.log('Update result:', result))
   .catch(err => console.error(err));
```

Example: Update Using findByIdAndUpdate:

javascript

```javascript
User.findByIdAndUpdate('USER_ID_HERE', { age: 27 }, { new: true })
   .then(user => console.log('Updated user:', user))
   .catch(err => console.error(err));
```

3.4 Delete Documents

Use .deleteOne() or .findByIdAndDelete() to remove documents.

Example: Delete a User by Email:

javascript

```javascript
User.deleteOne({ email: 'bob@example.com' })
   .then(result => console.log('Delete result:', result))
   .catch(err => console.error(err));
```

Example: Delete Using findByIdAndDelete:

javascript

```
User.findByIdAndDelete('USER_ID_HERE')
   .then(user => console.log('Deleted user:', user))
   .catch(err => console.error(err));
```

---

4. Designing Relationships in MongoDB

4.1 One-to-One Relationship

Store related data in the same document or as references.

Example: User and Profile Schema:

javascript

```
const profileSchema = new mongoose.Schema({
   bio: String,
   website: String,
   userId: { type: mongoose.Schema.Types.ObjectId, ref: 'User' },
});

const Profile = mongoose.model('Profile', profileSchema);
```

4.2 One-to-Many Relationship

Link documents using arrays of references.

Example: User and Posts Schema:

javascript

```javascript
const postSchema = new mongoose.Schema({
    title: String,
    content: String,
    userId: { type: mongoose.Schema.Types.ObjectId, ref: 'User' },
});

const Post = mongoose.model('Post', postSchema);
```

Populate Example:

Retrieve a user and their posts:

javascript

```javascript
User.findById('USER_ID_HERE')
    .populate('posts')
    .then(user => console.log('User with posts:', user))
    .catch(err => console.error(err));
```

4.3 Many-to-Many Relationship

Use arrays of references to connect multiple documents.

Example: Courses and Students Schema:

javascript

```javascript
const courseSchema = new mongoose.Schema({
    name: String,
    students: [{ type: mongoose.Schema.Types.ObjectId, ref: 'User' }],
});
```

```
const Course = mongoose.model('Course', courseSchema);
```

5. Best Practices for MongoDB Integration

1. **Define Schemas Carefully:**
   - Add validations and default values where applicable.

2. **Use Indexes:**
   - Optimize queries by creating indexes on frequently queried fields.

3. **Error Handling:**
   - Always handle errors using .catch() or try-catch blocks.

4. **Optimize Queries:**
   - Use .select() to retrieve only required fields.

5. **Leverage Middleware:**
   - Use schema middleware (pre and post) for actions like logging or validation.

6. Real-World Use Case: Building a Blog Application

1. **Schemas:**
   - User: Stores user details.
   - Post: Stores blog posts with references to the author.

o   Comment: Stores comments with references to the post and user.

2. **Operations:**

    o   Create a new post linked to a user.

    o   Fetch all posts with their authors and comments.

Integrating MongoDB with Node.js using Mongoose simplifies database operations, schema design, and relationship management. By mastering CRUD operations and schema relationships, you can build dynamic and scalable applications with MongoDB. The next chapter will explore working with relational databases like MySQL in Node.js.

Chapter 16: Authentication and Authorization

Overview

Authentication and authorization are critical components of web application security. Authentication verifies the identity of users, while authorization determines what resources users can access. This chapter focuses on implementing authentication with JSON Web Tokens (JWT), role-based access control, and OAuth for third-party authentication.

---

1. Authentication vs. Authorization

Authentication:

- Verifies the identity of a user.
- Examples: Login with username/password, biometrics, or single sign-on (SSO).

Authorization:

- Determines the level of access a user has after authentication.
- Examples: Admin vs. regular user privileges.

---

2. Implementing User Authentication with JWT

What is JWT?

- JSON Web Token (JWT) is an open standard for securely transmitting information between parties.
- JWTs are compact, URL-safe, and self-contained.

Structure of a JWT:

1. **Header:** Contains the type (JWT) and signing algorithm.

   json

   { "alg": "HS256", "typ": "JWT" }

2. **Payload:** Contains user data (claims).

   json

   { "userId": "12345", "role": "admin" }

3. **Signature:** A hash of the header and payload, signed with a secret or private key.

Flow of JWT Authentication:

1. The user logs in with credentials.
2. The server verifies credentials and generates a JWT.

3. The JWT is sent to the client and stored (e.g., in local storage or cookies).

4. The client includes the JWT in subsequent requests (e.g., in the Authorization header).

5. The server validates the JWT before granting access to protected routes.

Setting Up JWT Authentication
Step 1: Install Dependencies

bash

npm install jsonwebtoken bcryptjs express

Step 2: Create a User Model Simulate a database for demonstration purposes.

javascript

```
const bcrypt = require('bcryptjs');
let users = []; // In-memory user store for simplicity
```

Step 3: Create JWT Token

javascript

```
const jwt = require('jsonwebtoken');
const secretKey = 'your_secret_key';

// Generate JWT
```

```javascript
function generateToken(user) {
    return jwt.sign({ userId: user.id, role: user.role }, secretKey, { expiresIn: '1h'
});
}
```

Step 4: Register a New User Hash the password before storing it.

javascript

```javascript
const express = require('express');
const app = express();
app.use(express.json());

app.post('/register', async (req, res) => {
    const { username, password, role } = req.body;
    const hashedPassword = await bcrypt.hash(password, 10);
    const newUser = { id: Date.now(), username, password: hashedPassword, role
};
    users.push(newUser);
    res.status(201).send('User registered successfully!');
});
```

Step 5: User Login Validate credentials and generate a token.

javascript

```javascript
app.post('/login', async (req, res) => {
    const { username, password } = req.body;
    const user = users.find(u => u.username === username);
    if (!user) return res.status(404).send('User not found');

    const isPasswordValid = await bcrypt.compare(password, user.password);
    if (!isPasswordValid) return res.status(401).send('Invalid credentials');
```

```
const token = generateToken(user);
res.json({ token });
});
```

Step 6: Protect Routes with Middleware Verify the JWT for protected routes.

javascript

```
function authenticateToken(req, res, next) {
    const token = req.headers['authorization'];
    if (!token) return res.status(401).send('Access denied');

    jwt.verify(token, secretKey, (err, user) => {
        if (err) return res.status(403).send('Invalid token');
        req.user = user;
        next();
    });
}

// Example of a protected route
app.get('/protected', authenticateToken, (req, res) => {
    res.send('Welcome to the protected route!');
});
```

3. Role-Based Access Control (RBAC)

What is RBAC?

RBAC restricts access to resources based on user roles (e.g., admin, editor, viewer).

Implementing RBAC

Modify the middleware to check user roles.

javascript

```javascript
function authorizeRoles(...roles) {
   return (req, res, next) => {
      if (!roles.includes(req.user.role)) {
         return res.status(403).send('Access denied');
      }
      next();
   };
}

// Example: Protecting an admin route
app.get('/admin', authenticateToken, authorizeRoles('admin'), (req, res) => {
   res.send('Welcome, Admin!');
});
```

4. OAuth for Third-Party Authentication

What is OAuth?

OAuth is a standard for third-party authorization, allowing users to log in using platforms like Google, Facebook, or GitHub without sharing their credentials.

OAuth Flow:

1. The user clicks a "Login with Google" button.
2. The app redirects the user to Google for authentication.
3. Google prompts the user for consent and returns an authorization code.
4. The app exchanges the code for an access token.
5. The app uses the token to access user data.

Using Passport.js for OAuth

Passport.js is a popular middleware for authentication.

Step 1: Install Dependencies

bash

npm install passport passport-google-oauth20 express-session

Step 2: Configure Passport with Google Strategy

javascript

```javascript
const passport = require('passport');
const GoogleStrategy = require('passport-google-oauth20').Strategy;

passport.use(new GoogleStrategy({
    clientID: 'YOUR_GOOGLE_CLIENT_ID',
    clientSecret: 'YOUR_GOOGLE_CLIENT_SECRET',
    callbackURL: '/auth/google/callback',
}, (accessToken, refreshToken, profile, done) => {
    // Save user profile to database or session
```

```
      done(null, profile);
}));
```

```
passport.serializeUser((user, done) => done(null, user));
passport.deserializeUser((user, done) => done(null, user));
```

Step 3: Initialize Passport

javascript

```
const session = require('express-session');
app.use(session({ secret: 'your_secret_key', resave: false, saveUninitialized: true
}));
app.use(passport.initialize());
app.use(passport.session());
```

Step 4: Define Routes

javascript

```
// Redirect to Google for authentication
app.get('/auth/google', passport.authenticate('google', { scope: ['profile', 'email']
}));
```

```
// Handle Google callback
app.get('/auth/google/callback', passport.authenticate('google', { failureRedirect:
'/' }),
   (req, res) => {
      res.send('Logged in with Google!');
   }
);
```

5. Best Practices for Authentication and Authorization

1. **Use HTTPS:** Always secure your application with HTTPS to protect user data.

2. **Secure JWTs:** Store tokens securely in cookies with the HttpOnly and Secure flags.

3. **Implement Token Expiry:** Use short-lived tokens and refresh tokens for prolonged sessions.

4. **Log Suspicious Activity:** Monitor failed login attempts and notify users of unusual activity.

5. **Follow the Principle of Least Privilege:** Assign users the minimum permissions needed for their role.

Authentication and authorization are essential for securing web applications. JWT enables stateless authentication, while RBAC enforces granular access control. Additionally, OAuth facilitates seamless third-party authentication for users. By mastering these techniques, you can build secure, user-friendly, and scalable applications. The next chapter will explore deploying full-stack applications to production environments.

Chapter 17: Building RESTful APIs

Overview

RESTful APIs (Representational State Transfer) are a standard for creating scalable, maintainable, and stateless interfaces for web applications. This chapter delves into the principles of RESTful API design, versioning, error handling, and best practices to ensure robust and developer-friendly APIs.

---

1. What is a RESTful API?

Definition:

A RESTful API adheres to the principles of REST architecture, using HTTP methods to perform operations on resources.

Key Characteristics:

1. **Stateless:** Each request is independent and contains all the information needed to process it.
2. **Resource-Oriented:** API endpoints represent resources (e.g., /users, /products).
3. **HTTP Methods:** CRUD operations are mapped to HTTP methods:
   - o **GET:** Retrieve resources.
   - o **POST:** Create resources.

- o **PUT/PATCH:** Update resources.

- o **DELETE:** Remove resources.

4. **JSON Response:** Data is commonly exchanged in JSON format.

5. **Uniform Interface:** Consistent naming conventions and structure across endpoints.

---

2. Principles of RESTful API Design

2.1 Resource-Based URLs

- Use nouns to represent resources and avoid verbs.

  http

  GET /users
  POST /orders

2.2 HTTP Methods

- Leverage HTTP methods for CRUD operations:
  - o GET to retrieve data.
  - o POST to create new resources.
  - o PUT or PATCH to update existing resources.
  - o DELETE to remove resources.

2.3 Response Codes

- Use appropriate HTTP status codes to indicate the outcome:
  - o 200 OK for successful operations.
  - o 201 Created when a resource is created.
  - o 400 Bad Request for invalid input.
  - o 404 Not Found when the resource is missing.
  - o 500 Internal Server Error for server-side issues.

2.4 Pagination and Filtering

- For large datasets, implement pagination and filtering.

  http

  GET /products?category=electronics&page=2&limit=10

2.5 Statelessness

- Each request should contain all required data (e.g., authentication tokens) and avoid maintaining session state on the server.

---

3. Setting Up a RESTful API

Step 1: Initialize the Project
bash

mkdir restful-api

```
cd restful-api
npm init -y
npm install express mongoose
```

Step 2: Define a Resource

Example: Managing users.

Schema Definition:

javascript

```javascript
const mongoose = require('mongoose');

const userSchema = new mongoose.Schema({
    name: { type: String, required: true },
    email: { type: String, required: true, unique: true },
    age: { type: Number, min: 0 },
});

const User = mongoose.model('User', userSchema);
module.exports = User;
```

Step 3: Create Routes

User Routes:

javascript

```javascript
const express = require('express');
const User = require('./models/user');
const router = express.Router();
```

```
// Get all users
router.get('/users', async (req, res) => {
    const users = await User.find();
    res.status(200).json(users);
});

// Get a user by ID
router.get('/users/:id', async (req, res) => {
    try {
        const user = await User.findById(req.params.id);
        if (!user) return res.status(404).json({ error: 'User not found' });
        res.status(200).json(user);
    } catch (err) {
        res.status(500).json({ error: 'Server error' });
    }
});

// Create a new user
router.post('/users', async (req, res) => {
    try {
        const newUser = await User.create(req.body);
        res.status(201).json(newUser);
    } catch (err) {
        res.status(400).json({ error: 'Invalid input' });
    }
});

// Update a user
router.put('/users/:id', async (req, res) => {
    try {
```

```javascript
    const   updatedUser   =   await   User.findByIdAndUpdate(req.params.id,
req.body, { new: true });
      if (!updatedUser) return res.status(404).json({ error: 'User not found' });
      res.status(200).json(updatedUser);
    } catch (err) {
      res.status(400).json({ error: 'Invalid input' });
    }
});


// Delete a user
router.delete('/users/:id', async (req, res) => {
    try {
      const deletedUser = await User.findByIdAndDelete(req.params.id);
      if (!deletedUser) return res.status(404).json({ error: 'User not found' });
      res.status(200).json({ message: 'User deleted' });
    } catch (err) {
      res.status(500).json({ error: 'Server error' });
    }
});


module.exports = router;
```

Step 4: Integrate Routes into the App

javascript

```javascript
const express = require('express');
const mongoose = require('mongoose');
const userRoutes = require('./routes/users');


const app = express();
app.use(express.json());
```

```
app.use('/api', userRoutes);

mongoose.connect('mongodb://localhost:27017/restful-api', { useNewUrlParser:
true, useUnifiedTopology: true });

app.listen(3000, () => {
   console.log('Server is running on http://localhost:3000');
});
```

---

4. Versioning Your API

Why Version APIs?

- Allow changes or improvements without breaking existing clients.
- Example: /api/v1/users vs. /api/v2/users.

How to Implement Versioning:

1. Use URL versioning:

   http

   GET /api/v1/users

2. Use headers for versioning:

   http

```
GET /users
Accept: application/vnd.api.v1+json
```

---

5. Error Handling in RESTful APIs

Standard Error Format:

Provide consistent error responses:

json

```json
{
  "error": {
    "message": "Invalid input",
    "code": 400,
    "details": "Email is required"
  }
}
```

Error Handling Middleware:

Centralize error handling:

javascript

```javascript
app.use((err, req, res, next) => {
  console.error(err.stack);
  res.status(500).json({ error: 'Something went wrong!' });
});
```

---

6. Best Practices for RESTful APIs

1. **Use Proper HTTP Methods:** Stick to the standard CRUD-to-HTTP method mappings.
2. **Paginate Large Responses:** Use query parameters like page and limit.
3. **Secure the API:**
   - Use HTTPS.
   - Authenticate requests using tokens (e.g., JWT).
4. **Document the API:** Tools like Swagger or Postman can help document API endpoints.
5. **Return Useful Status Codes:** Ensure your API conveys the correct meaning through status codes.
6. **Validate Input:** Use libraries like Joi or express-validator to validate user input.

---

7. Tools for RESTful API Development

Tool	Purpose
Postman	API testing and debugging.
Swagger/OpenAPI	API documentation and testing.
Insomnia	API design and debugging.

Tool	Purpose
Express.js	Framework for building RESTful APIs in Node.js.

RESTful APIs are the backbone of modern web and mobile applications. By following principles like resource-based design, proper HTTP methods, and consistent error handling, you can build APIs that are robust, maintainable, and developer-friendly. In the next chapter, we will explore advanced deployment strategies for full-stack applications.

Chapter 18: GraphQL Basics

Overview

GraphQL is a powerful query language and runtime for APIs, designed to overcome the limitations of REST. It allows clients to request precisely the data they need, making APIs more flexible and efficient. This chapter explores the differences between REST and GraphQL, and demonstrates how to build a GraphQL API using Apollo Server.

---

1. What is GraphQL?

Definition:

GraphQL is a query language for APIs that provides a more flexible and efficient alternative to REST. Developed by Facebook, it allows clients to define the structure of the required data and retrieve multiple resources in a single request.

Key Features:

1. **Single Endpoint:** Unlike REST, which uses multiple endpoints, GraphQL uses a single endpoint for all queries and mutations.
2. **Exact Data Retrieval:** Clients can specify exactly the data they need, reducing over-fetching or under-fetching.

3. **Schema-Based:** APIs are defined by a strongly typed schema, improving predictability and validation.
4. **Real-Time Updates:** Supports subscriptions for real-time data.

2. Comparing REST and GraphQL

Feature	REST	GraphQL
Data Retrieval	Multiple endpoints for different resources.	Single endpoint with custom queries.
Over-fetching	Fetches all fields of a resource.	Returns only requested fields.
Under-fetching	Requires multiple requests for related data.	Combines related data in one request.
Schema	Not strictly defined.	Strongly typed schema defines the API.
Real-Time Support	Limited (e.g., WebSockets for REST).	Built-in subscriptions for real-time data.

3. Setting Up a GraphQL API with Apollo Server

Step 1: Install Dependencies

bash

npm install apollo-server graphql

Step 2: Define a Schema

GraphQL schemas define the structure of queries, mutations, and types.

Example Schema:

javascript

```
const { gql } = require('apollo-server');

const typeDefs = gql`
  type User {
    id: ID!
    name: String!
    email: String!
  }

  type Query {
    users: [User!]!
    user(id: ID!): User
  }

  type Mutation {
    createUser(name: String!, email: String!): User
  }
`;
```

Step 3: Create Resolvers

Resolvers define how the data is fetched or modified.

Example Resolvers:

javascript

```
const users = [];

const resolvers = {
  Query: {
    users: () => users,
    user: (_, { id }) => users.find(user => user.id === id),
  },
  Mutation: {
    createUser: (_, { name, email }) => {
      const user = { id: `${Date.now()}`, name, email };
      users.push(user);
      return user;
    },
  },
};
```

Step 4: Set Up Apollo Server

Combine the schema and resolvers to create the server.

Example:

javascript

```javascript
const { ApolloServer } = require('apollo-server');

const typeDefs = gql`
  type User {
    id: ID!
    name: String!
    email: String!
  }

  type Query {
    users: [User!]!
    user(id: ID!): User
  }

  type Mutation {
    createUser(name: String!, email: String!): User
  }
`;

const resolvers = {
  Query: {
    users: () => users,
    user: (_, { id }) => users.find(user => user.id === id),
  },
  Mutation: {
    createUser: (_, { name, email }) => {
      const user = { id: `${Date.now()}`, name, email };
      users.push(user);
```

```
    return user;
  },
 },
};
```

```
const server = new ApolloServer({ typeDefs, resolvers });
```

```
server.listen().then(({ url }) => {
  console.log(`🚀 Server ready at ${url}`);
});
```

---

4. Testing the GraphQL API

Step 1: Launch the Server
Run the server:

bash

node index.js

Step 2: Access the GraphQL Playground
Navigate to the provided URL (e.g., http://localhost:4000) to open the GraphQL Playground.

Step 3: Execute Queries and Mutations
Query: Fetch All Users

graphql

```
query {
 users {
  id
  name
  email
 }
}
```

Query: Fetch a User by ID

graphql

```
query {
 user(id: "12345") {
  name
  email
 }
}
```

Mutation: Create a New User

graphql

```
mutation {
 createUser(name: "Alice", email: "alice@example.com") {
  id
  name
  email
 }
}
```

5. Real-Time Data with Subscriptions

What are Subscriptions?

Subscriptions in GraphQL enable real-time updates by pushing data to clients when specific events occur.

Example: Adding Subscriptions

Install graphql-subscriptions:

bash

npm install graphql-subscriptions

Modify the server to include subscriptions:

javascript

```
const { PubSub } = require('graphql-subscriptions');
const pubsub = new PubSub();
const USER_CREATED = 'USER_CREATED';

const typeDefs = gql`
  type User {
    id: ID!
    name: String!
    email: String!
  }

  type Query {
    users: [User!]!
  }
```

```
type Mutation {
  createUser(name: String!, email: String!): User
}

type Subscription {
  userCreated: User
}
`;

const resolvers = {
  Query: {
    users: () => users,
  },
  Mutation: {
    createUser: (_, { name, email }) => {
      const user = { id: `${Date.now()}`, name, email };
      users.push(user);
      pubsub.publish(USER_CREATED, { userCreated: user });
      return user;
    },
  },
  Subscription: {
    userCreated: {
      subscribe: () => pubsub.asyncIterator([USER_CREATED]),
    },
  },
};

const { ApolloServer } = require('apollo-server');
```

```
const server = new ApolloServer({ typeDefs, resolvers });
server.listen().then(({ url }) => {
  console.log(`🚀 Server ready at ${url}`);
});
```

6. Best Practices for Building GraphQL APIs

1. **Design Granular Queries:** Allow clients to fetch only the fields they need.
2. **Paginate Data:** Avoid fetching large datasets by implementing pagination.
3. **Secure the API:**
   o Use authentication and authorization for sensitive operations.
   o Validate input data.
4. **Optimize Resolvers:** Avoid over-fetching from the database by optimizing resolver logic.
5. **Monitor Performance:** Use tools like Apollo Studio to monitor query performance and errors.

GraphQL is a versatile alternative to REST, providing clients with more control over the data they fetch and enabling real-time communication through subscriptions. By building a GraphQL API with Apollo Server, developers can create scalable and flexible APIs that enhance the client-server interaction. The next chapter will delve into deploying full-stack applications with modern cloud services.

Chapter 19: Real-Time Communication with WebSockets

Overview

Real-time communication is essential for applications like chat systems, live notifications, collaborative tools, and gaming. WebSockets provide a persistent connection between the client and server, enabling real-time data exchange. This chapter focuses on implementing real-time features using Socket.io and building a simple chat application.

---

1. What are WebSockets?

Definition:

WebSockets are a protocol for two-way communication between a client and a server over a single, long-lived connection.

Key Features:

- **Full-Duplex Communication:** Allows both the client and server to send messages independently.
- **Low Latency:** Reduces overhead compared to HTTP-based communication.
- **Persistent Connection:** Maintains a continuous connection, ideal for real-time applications.

WebSockets vs. HTTP:

Feature	WebSockets	HTTP
Connection	Persistent	Stateless (new connection per request).
Communication	Bidirectional	Request-response only.
Latency	Low	Higher due to connection overhead.
Use Cases	Chat, gaming, real-time notifications	Static websites, APIs.

2. What is Socket.io?

Definition:

Socket.io is a JavaScript library built on WebSockets. It simplifies real-time communication by providing:

- Automatic reconnection handling.
- Event-based communication.
- Cross-browser compatibility.

Why Use Socket.io?

- Easy integration with Node.js.

- Built-in fallbacks for environments that do not support WebSockets.
- Flexible event-driven architecture.

---

3. Setting Up Socket.io

Step 1: Install Dependencies

bash

```
npm install socket.io express
```

Step 2: Create a Basic Server

Set up a Node.js server using Express and Socket.io:

javascript

```javascript
const express = require('express');
const http = require('http');
const { Server } = require('socket.io');

const app = express();
const server = http.createServer(app);
const io = new Server(server);

app.get('/', (req, res) => {
    res.sendFile(__dirname + '/index.html');
});
```

```
io.on('connection', (socket) => {
    console.log('A user connected');
    socket.on('disconnect', () => {
        console.log('User disconnected');
    });
});


server.listen(3000, () => {
    console.log('Server running on http://localhost:3000');
});
```

Step 3: Create the Client Side

Create an index.html file for the client:

html

```
<!DOCTYPE html>
<html>
<head>
    <title>Socket.io Chat</title>
</head>
<body>
    <h1>Welcome to the Chat App</h1>
    <script src="/socket.io/socket.io.js"></script>
    <script>
        const socket = io();
    </script>
</body>
</html>
```

4. Building a Chat Application

4.1 Basic Chat Application

Server-Side Code: Modify the server to handle chat messages:

javascript

```javascript
io.on('connection', (socket) => {
  console.log('A user connected');

  // Listen for chat messages
  socket.on('chat message', (msg) => {
    console.log('Message received:', msg);
    io.emit('chat message', msg); // Broadcast message to all clients
  });

  socket.on('disconnect', () => {
    console.log('User disconnected');
  });
});
```

Client-Side Code: Enhance the client to send and display messages:

html

```html
<!DOCTYPE html>
<html>
<head>
  <title>Chat App</title>
</head>
<body>
  <h1>Chat App</h1>
```

```
<ul id="messages"></ul>
<form id="form" action="">
    <input id="input" autocomplete="off" /><button>Send</button>
</form>
<script src="/socket.io/socket.io.js"></script>
<script>
    const socket = io();

    // Listen for form submission
    const form = document.getElementById('form');
    const input = document.getElementById('input');
    const messages = document.getElementById('messages');

    form.addEventListener('submit', (e) => {
        e.preventDefault();
        if (input.value) {
            socket.emit('chat message', input.value);
            input.value = '';
        }
    });

    // Listen for messages from the server
    socket.on('chat message', (msg) => {
        const li = document.createElement('li');
        li.textContent = msg;
        messages.appendChild(li);
    });
</script>
</body>
</html>
```

4.2 Real-Time Notifications

Add real-time notifications for user connections and disconnections:

javascript

```javascript
io.on('connection', (socket) => {
    io.emit('notification', 'A new user has joined the chat');

    socket.on('disconnect', () => {
        io.emit('notification', 'A user has left the chat');
    });
});
```

Client-Side Code for Notifications:

javascript

```javascript
socket.on('notification', (msg) => {
    const li = document.createElement('li');
    li.textContent = msg;
    li.style.color = 'gray';
    messages.appendChild(li);
});
```

---

5. Advanced Features with Socket.io

5.1 Private Messaging

Add functionality for direct messages between users:

- Assign each user a unique socket.id on connection.

- Use socket.to(<socket_id>).emit('event', data) for private messages.

5.2 Rooms

Organize users into chat rooms:

javascript

```javascript
socket.on('join room', (room) => {
  socket.join(room);
  io.to(room).emit('notification', `A user joined room: ${room}`);
});
```

5.3 Broadcasting Events

Send messages to all clients except the sender:

javascript

```javascript
socket.broadcast.emit('event', 'This is a broadcast message');
```

5.4 Typing Indicators

Notify users when someone is typing:

javascript

```javascript
socket.on('typing', (username) => {
  socket.broadcast.emit('typing', `${username} is typing...`);
});
```

---

6. Securing Real-Time Applications

1. **Validate Input:** Sanitize and validate all messages to prevent injection attacks.

2. **Authenticate Users:** Use tokens (e.g., JWT) for secure connections.

3. **Use Namespaces:** Separate sensitive and public communications.

javascript

```
const secureNamespace = io.of('/secure');
```

4. **Rate Limiting:** Prevent abuse by limiting the number of messages a user can send in a given time.

---

7. Real-World Use Cases for WebSockets

1. **Chat Applications:** Real-time messaging and notifications.
2. **Live Feeds:** Sports updates, news tickers.
3. **Collaborative Tools:** Shared document editing.
4. **Gaming:** Multiplayer online games.
5. **IoT Applications:** Real-time device monitoring.

WebSockets and Socket.io enable developers to build real-time, bidirectional communication features with ease. By mastering these technologies, you can create dynamic applications like chat systems, collaborative tools, and live notifications. The next chapter will explore deploying full-stack applications in production environments.

Chapter 20: Testing and Debugging

Overview

Testing and debugging are crucial for building reliable and maintainable web applications. Writing tests ensures that your code behaves as expected, while debugging helps identify and resolve issues. This chapter explores writing unit tests with **Jest** and **Mocha**, along with debugging techniques and tools for modern web development.

---

1. Importance of Testing and Debugging

Why Test?

- Ensures code correctness and prevents regressions.
- Improves code maintainability and reliability.
- Builds confidence when deploying new features or updates.

Why Debug?

- Identifies and resolves bugs during development.
- Enhances the performance and functionality of your application.
- Reduces downtime in production systems.

2. Writing Unit Tests with Jest

What is Jest?

- A JavaScript testing framework developed by Facebook.
- Works seamlessly with modern JavaScript applications (React, Node.js).
- Supports features like mocks, snapshots, and code coverage.

Setting Up Jest:

1. Install Jest:

bash

```
npm install --save-dev jest
```

2. Add a test script to your package.json:

json

```
{
  "scripts": {
    "test": "jest"
  }
}
```

Writing Tests with Jest:

Example: Testing a Calculator Function

javascript

```javascript
// calculator.js
function add(a, b) {
    return a + b;
}

function subtract(a, b) {
    return a - b;
}

module.exports = { add, subtract };
```

Test File:

javascript

```javascript
// calculator.test.js
const { add, subtract } = require('./calculator');

test('adds two numbers', () => {
    expect(add(2, 3)).toBe(5);
});

test('subtracts two numbers', () => {
    expect(subtract(5, 3)).toBe(2);
});
```

Running Tests:

bash

```bash
npm test
```

Mocking Functions:

Mock external dependencies or services:

javascript

```
const fetchData = jest.fn(() => Promise.resolve('data'));

test('fetches data successfully', async () => {
   const data = await fetchData();
   expect(data).toBe('data');
});
```

---

3. Writing Unit Tests with Mocha

What is Mocha?

- A flexible JavaScript test framework.
- Often used with assertion libraries like **Chai**.

Setting Up Mocha:

1. Install Mocha and Chai:

   bash

   npm install --save-dev mocha chai

2. Add a test script to your package.json:

json

```json
{
  "scripts": {
    "test": "mocha"
  }
}
```

Writing Tests with Mocha and Chai:

Example: Testing a Calculator Function

javascript

```javascript
// calculator.js
function multiply(a, b) {
   return a * b;
}

module.exports = { multiply };
```

Test File:

javascript

```javascript
// calculator.test.js
const { expect } = require('chai');
const { multiply } = require('./calculator');

describe('Calculator', () => {
   it('multiplies two numbers', () => {
      expect(multiply(2, 3)).to.equal(6);
   });
```

```
});
```

Running Tests:

bash

npm test

---

4. Debugging Tools and Techniques

4.1 Debugging with console.log

- Simplest way to debug.
- Use strategically to inspect variables or program flow.

javascript

```
console.log('Value of x:', x);
```

4.2 Using Node.js Debugger

1. Add the debugger keyword to your code:

javascript

```
function testDebugger() {
    let x = 10;
    debugger; // Program stops here in debug mode
    x++;
    return x;
}
```

```
testDebugger();
```

2. Run in debug mode:

```bash
bash
```

```
node inspect app.js
```

4.3 Debugging in Visual Studio Code

- VS Code has an integrated debugger for Node.js and browser-based applications.

1. Add a launch.json configuration:

```json
json
```

```json
{
   "configurations": [
      {
         "type": "node",
         "request": "launch",
         "name": "Launch Program",
         "program": "${workspaceFolder}/app.js"
      }
   ]
}
```

2. Set breakpoints in your code.
3. Press F5 to start debugging.

4.4 Browser Developer Tools

1. Open DevTools in Chrome or Edge (Ctrl+Shift+I or Cmd+Option+I on macOS).
2. Use the **Sources** tab to:
   - o Set breakpoints.
   - o Step through code.
   - o Inspect variables and the call stack.

---

5. Advanced Debugging Techniques

5.1 Error Stack Traces

- Analyze error stack traces to locate issues in your code.

javascript

```
try {
    throw new Error('Something went wrong!');
} catch (err) {
    console.error(err.stack);
}
```

5.2 Using Linters

- Tools like ESLint help catch syntax errors and enforce code standards before runtime.

```bash
```

```
npm install eslint --save-dev
```

5.3 Monitoring Logs

- Use logging libraries like Winston or Morgan for structured logs.

```bash
```

```
npm install winston
```

5.4 Performance Profiling

- Use the **Performance** tab in browser DevTools to identify slow-running code.
- Node.js also has built-in performance profiling:

```bash
```

```
node --inspect-brk app.js
```

5.5 Debugging Memory Leaks

- Use tools like Chrome DevTools' **Memory** tab or Node.js' heapdump module.

```bash
```

```
npm install heapdump
```

6. Best Practices for Testing and Debugging

1. **Write Tests Early:** Adopt test-driven development (TDD) to guide the development process.

2. **Test Coverage:** Ensure comprehensive coverage for critical paths and edge cases.

3. **Automate Testing:** Use CI/CD pipelines to automate test execution.

4. **Use Meaningful Logs:** Log errors and application events for easier debugging.

5. **Document Known Issues:** Maintain a list of resolved and unresolved bugs for reference.

Testing and debugging are essential skills for delivering high-quality applications. By using tools like Jest and Mocha for unit testing and leveraging powerful debugging techniques and tools, developers can identify and resolve issues efficiently. The next chapter will cover deploying full-stack applications to production environments.

Chapter 21: Deploying Applications

Overview

Deploying applications involves making your code accessible to users by hosting it on a server or cloud platform. This chapter covers popular hosting options like **Heroku**, **Netlify**, and **AWS**, and provides guidance on setting up **Continuous Integration/Continuous Deployment (CI/CD)** pipelines to streamline deployments.

---

1. Hosting Options

1.1 Heroku
What is Heroku?

- A platform-as-a-service (PaaS) that simplifies deployment and scaling of web applications.
- Supports multiple programming languages.

Steps to Deploy with Heroku:

1. **Install Heroku CLI:**

   bash

   ```
   npm install -g heroku
   ```

2. **Log in to Heroku:**

bash

heroku login

3. **Create a Heroku App:**

bash

heroku create

4. **Push Code to Heroku:**
   - o Add a Procfile to specify the start command:

     makefile

     web: node app.js

   - o Push code to Heroku:

     bash

     git push heroku main

5. **Visit Your App:** Heroku provides a unique URL for your app (e.g., https://your-app-name.herokuapp.com).

1.2 Netlify

What is Netlify?

- A hosting platform optimized for static websites and serverless functions.
- Provides features like custom domains, HTTPS, and continuous deployment.

Steps to Deploy with Netlify:

1. **Sign Up:** Create an account at Netlify.
2. **Link Repository:**
   - Connect your GitHub, GitLab, or Bitbucket repository.
3. **Configure Build Settings:**
   - Specify the build command (e.g., npm run build) and publish directory (e.g., dist or build).
4. **Deploy:** Netlify automatically deploys the site after the build completes.
5. **Custom Domain:**
   - Add a custom domain through the Netlify dashboard.

1.3 AWS

What is AWS?

- Amazon Web Services (AWS) is a cloud computing platform that offers various services for deploying and managing applications.

Common AWS Services for Deployment:

1. **Amazon S3:** Host static websites.
2. **AWS Elastic Beanstalk:** Simplified deployment for full-stack applications.
3. **AWS Lambda:** Serverless functions.
4. **Amazon EC2:** Virtual servers for flexible deployment.

Deploying with AWS Elastic Beanstalk:

1. **Install AWS CLI:**

bash

pip install awscli

2. **Initialize Elastic Beanstalk:**

bash

eb init

3. **Create and Deploy:**

bash

```
eb create my-app-env
eb deploy
```

---

2. Setting Up CI/CD Pipelines

What is CI/CD?

- **Continuous Integration (CI):** Automates the testing and integration of code changes.
- **Continuous Deployment (CD):** Automatically deploys tested changes to production.

Benefits of CI/CD:

1. Reduces manual errors during deployment.
2. Speeds up the release cycle.
3. Ensures consistent testing and deployment processes.

2.1 Setting Up CI/CD with GitHub Actions
What are GitHub Actions?

- GitHub Actions enable automation workflows directly within GitHub repositories.

Example Workflow:

1. Create a .github/workflows/deploy.yml **file:**

yaml

name: CI/CD Pipeline

```yaml
on:
  push:
    branches:
      - main

jobs:
  build:
    runs-on: ubuntu-latest

    steps:
      - name: Checkout Code
        uses: actions/checkout@v3

      - name: Set up Node.js
        uses: actions/setup-node@v3
        with:
          node-version: '16'

      - name: Install Dependencies
        run: npm install

      - name: Run Tests
        run: npm test
```

```
- name: Build Application
  run: npm run build

- name: Deploy to Heroku
  env:
    HEROKU_API_KEY: ${{ secrets.HEROKU_API_KEY }}
  run: |
    heroku git:remote -a your-heroku-app
    git push heroku main
```

Steps to Configure:

1. Add HEROKU_API_KEY to your repository secrets.
2. Push changes to the main branch to trigger the workflow.

2.2 Setting Up CI/CD with Netlify

Netlify's Continuous Deployment:

1. Link your Git repository to Netlify.
2. Every push to the specified branch triggers a new deployment.
3. Use netlify.toml to customize build settings:

```toml
[build]
  command = "npm run build"
  publish = "build"
```

2.3 Setting Up CI/CD with AWS CodePipeline

What is AWS CodePipeline?

- A CI/CD service for automating the build, test, and deployment processes.

Steps to Configure CodePipeline:

1. **Create a Pipeline:**
   o Use the AWS Management Console to define source (e.g., GitHub), build (e.g., CodeBuild), and deploy (e.g., Elastic Beanstalk) stages.
2. **Define a Buildspec File:** Add a buildspec.yml file to your project:

yaml

version: 0.2

```
phases:
  install:
    commands:
      - npm install
  build:
    commands:
      - npm run build
artifacts:
```

files:
- '**/*'

---

3. Best Practices for Deployment

1. **Environment Variables:**
   - Store sensitive data (e.g., API keys) securely using environment variables.
   - Example in Node.js:

   javascript

   ```
   const apiKey = process.env.API_KEY;
   ```

2. **Automated Testing:**
   - Ensure all changes are tested before deployment.
3. **Monitor Deployments:**
   - Use tools like **AWS CloudWatch**, **Heroku Metrics**, or **Netlify Analytics** to monitor application health.
4. **Rollback Strategy:**
   - Have a plan to revert to a previous version in case of deployment failures.
5. **Optimize Build Artifacts:**
   - Minimize the size of files being deployed to improve performance.

---

4. Tools for Deployment

Tool	Purpose
Heroku	Simplified hosting for web applications.
Netlify	Optimized for static websites and serverless apps.
AWS Elastic Beanstalk	Automates deployment for scalable applications.
GitHub Actions	CI/CD pipelines integrated with GitHub.
AWS CodePipeline	CI/CD for complex AWS workflows.

Deploying applications effectively is critical to delivering a seamless user experience. Hosting options like Heroku, Netlify, and AWS offer flexibility and scalability, while CI/CD pipelines automate the deployment process, ensuring rapid and reliable updates. The next chapter will delve into optimizing performance and scaling full-stack applications.

Chapter 22: Building a Blogging Platform

Overview

A blogging platform is an excellent project to demonstrate full-stack development skills. This chapter guides you through building a simple blogging application with a **React** front-end and an **Express** back-end. It includes features like user authentication, CRUD (Create, Read, Update, Delete) operations for blog posts, and deployment to a production server.

---

1. Project Setup

1.1 Back-End Setup with Express
Step 1: Initialize the Project

bash

```
mkdir blogging-platform
cd blogging-platform
npm init -y
npm install express mongoose bcryptjs jsonwebtoken cors dotenv
```

Step 2: Directory Structure

bash

```
blogging-platform/
|
```

```
├── server/
│   ├── models/
│   ├── routes/
│   ├── .env
│   ├── app.js
│   └── server.js
```

Step 3: Configure the Server

javascript

```javascript
// server/app.js
const express = require('express');
const cors = require('cors');
const mongoose = require('mongoose');
require('dotenv').config();

const app = express();
app.use(cors());
app.use(express.json());

// Connect to MongoDB
mongoose.connect(process.env.MONGO_URI, {
    useNewUrlParser: true,
    useUnifiedTopology: true,
}).then(() => console.log('Connected to MongoDB'))
  .catch(err => console.error('MongoDB connection error:', err));

// Routes
app.use('/api/auth', require('./routes/auth'));
app.use('/api/posts', require('./routes/posts'));
```

```
module.exports = app;
```

Step 4: Create the Server

javascript

```
// server/server.js
const app = require('./app');

const PORT = process.env.PORT || 5000;

app.listen(PORT, () => {
    console.log(`Server running on http://localhost:${PORT}`);
});
```

---

2. Back-End Features

2.1 Authentication

Create the User Model:

javascript

```
// server/models/User.js
const mongoose = require('mongoose');
const bcrypt = require('bcryptjs');

const userSchema = new mongoose.Schema({
    username: { type: String, required: true, unique: true },
    password: { type: String, required: true },
});
```

```javascript
// Hash password before saving
userSchema.pre('save', async function (next) {
    if (!this.isModified('password')) return next();
    this.password = await bcrypt.hash(this.password, 10);
    next();
});


module.exports = mongoose.model('User', userSchema);
```

Auth Routes:

javascript

```javascript
// server/routes/auth.js
const express = require('express');
const jwt = require('jsonwebtoken');
const User = require('../models/User');
const router = express.Router();

// Register
router.post('/register', async (req, res) => {
    try {
        const user = new User(req.body);
        await user.save();
        res.status(201).json({ message: 'User registered' });
    } catch (err) {
        res.status(400).json({ error: err.message });
    }
});

// Login
router.post('/login', async (req, res) => {
```

```javascript
  try {
    const user = await User.findOne({ username: req.body.username });
    if (!user || !(await bcrypt.compare(req.body.password, user.password))) {
      return res.status(401).json({ error: 'Invalid credentials' });
    }
    const token = jwt.sign({ id: user._id }, process.env.JWT_SECRET, {
expiresIn: '1h' });
    res.json({ token });
  } catch (err) {
    res.status(400).json({ error: err.message });
  }
});

module.exports = router;
```

2.2 CRUD Operations

Create the Post Model:

javascript

```javascript
// server/models/Post.js
const mongoose = require('mongoose');

const postSchema = new mongoose.Schema({
  title: { type: String, required: true },
  content: { type: String, required: true },
  author: { type: mongoose.Schema.Types.ObjectId, ref: 'User', required: true },
  createdAt: { type: Date, default: Date.now },
});
```

```
module.exports = mongoose.model('Post', postSchema);
```

Post Routes:

javascript

```javascript
// server/routes/posts.js
const express = require('express');
const Post = require('../models/Post');
const jwt = require('jsonwebtoken');
const router = express.Router();

// Middleware to verify token
function authenticateToken(req, res, next) {
    const token = req.headers['authorization'];
    if (!token) return res.status(401).send('Access Denied');

    jwt.verify(token, process.env.JWT_SECRET, (err, user) => {
        if (err) return res.status(403).send('Invalid Token');
        req.user = user;
        next();
    });
}

// Get all posts
router.get('/', async (req, res) => {
    const posts = await Post.find().populate('author', 'username');
    res.json(posts);
});

// Create a post
router.post('/', authenticateToken, async (req, res) => {
```

```
const post = new Post({ ...req.body, author: req.user.id });
await post.save();
res.status(201).json(post);
});


// Update a post
router.put('/:id', authenticateToken, async (req, res) => {
  const post = await Post.findByIdAndUpdate(req.params.id, req.body, { new:
true });
  res.json(post);
});


// Delete a post
router.delete('/:id', authenticateToken, async (req, res) => {
  await Post.findByIdAndDelete(req.params.id);
  res.json({ message: 'Post deleted' });
});


module.exports = router;
```

3. Front-End Development with React

3.1 Setting Up the React App

bash

```
npx create-react-app blogging-platform-client
cd blogging-platform-client
npm install axios react-router-dom
```

3.2 Directory Structure

css

```
blogging-platform-client/
|
├── src/
|   ├── components/
|   ├── pages/
|   ├── App.js
|   └── index.js
```

3.3 Implementing Features

Create a Login Page:

javascript

```javascript
// src/pages/Login.js
import React, { useState } from 'react';
import axios from 'axios';

function Login() {
    const [formData, setFormData] = useState({ username: '', password: '' });

    const handleSubmit = async (e) => {
        e.preventDefault();
        try {
            const response = await axios.post('/api/auth/login', formData);
            localStorage.setItem('token', response.data.token);
            alert('Logged in successfully');
        } catch (error) {
            alert('Login failed');
```

```
    }
  };


  return (
    <form onSubmit={handleSubmit}>
      <input   type="text"   placeholder="Username"   onChange={(e)   =>
setFormData({ ...formData, username: e.target.value })} />
      <input type="password" placeholder="Password" onChange={(e) =>
setFormData({ ...formData, password: e.target.value })} />
      <button type="submit">Login</button>
    </form>
  );
}


export default Login;
```

Fetch Posts:

javascript

```
// src/pages/Posts.js
import React, { useEffect, useState } from 'react';
import axios from 'axios';


function Posts() {
  const [posts, setPosts] = useState([]);


  useEffect(() => {
    const fetchPosts = async () => {
      const response = await axios.get('/api/posts');
      setPosts(response.data);
    };
```

```
    fetchPosts();
  }, []);

  return (
    <div>
      {posts.map(post => (
        <div key={post._id}>
          <h2>{post.title}</h2>
          <p>{post.content}</p>
          <small>By {post.author.username}</small>
        </div>
      ))}
    </div>
  );
}
```

```
export default Posts;
```

4. Deployment

4.1 Deploying the Back-End

1. **Heroku Deployment:**

   bash

   ```
   heroku create
   git push heroku main
   ```

4.2 Deploying the Front-End

1. **Netlify Deployment:**
   o Build the React app:

   bash

   npm run build

   o Deploy the build folder to Netlify.

This blogging platform demonstrates the integration of a **React** front-end with an **Express** back-end, implementing core features like authentication, CRUD operations, and deployment. By following this guide, you gain hands-on experience building scalable full-stack applications. The next chapter will explore advanced techniques for optimizing full-stack projects.

Chapter 23: Building an E-Commerce Website

Overview

An e-commerce website combines multiple functionalities to provide users with a seamless shopping experience. This chapter focuses on building a full-stack e-commerce application with features like product catalogs, shopping carts, and secure payment systems. It also explores integrating third-party APIs for payments and shipping.

---

1. Project Setup

1.1 Back-End Setup

Use **Node.js** with **Express** for the server and **MongoDB** as the database.

Install Dependencies:

bash

```
mkdir e-commerce
cd e-commerce
npm init -y
npm install express mongoose bcryptjs jsonwebtoken stripe cors dotenv
```

Directory Structure:

bash

```
e-commerce/
|
├── server/
|   ├── models/
|   ├── routes/
|   ├── controllers/
|   ├── .env
|   ├── app.js
|   └── server.js
```

Server Configuration:

javascript

```javascript
// server/app.js
const express = require('express');
const mongoose = require('mongoose');
const cors = require('cors');
require('dotenv').config();

const app = express();
app.use(cors());
app.use(express.json());

mongoose.connect(process.env.MONGO_URI, {
    useNewUrlParser: true,
    useUnifiedTopology: true,
}).then(() => console.log('MongoDB Connected'))
  .catch(err => console.error(err));
```

```
// Routes
app.use('/api/products', require('./routes/products'));
app.use('/api/cart', require('./routes/cart'));
app.use('/api/checkout', require('./routes/checkout'));

module.exports = app;
```

Start the Server:

javascript

```
// server/server.js
const app = require('./app');
const PORT = process.env.PORT || 5000;

app.listen(PORT, () => {
    console.log(`Server running at http://localhost:${PORT}`);
});
```

---

2. Back-End Features

2.1 Product Catalog

Product Model:

javascript

```
// server/models/Product.js
const mongoose = require('mongoose');

const productSchema = new mongoose.Schema({
    name: { type: String, required: true },
```

```
    description: { type: String },
    price: { type: Number, required: true },
    stock: { type: Number, required: true },
    image: { type: String },
});
```

```
module.exports = mongoose.model('Product', productSchema);
```

Product Routes:

javascript

```javascript
// server/routes/products.js
const express = require('express');
const Product = require('../models/Product');
const router = express.Router();

// Get all products
router.get('/', async (req, res) => {
    const products = await Product.find();
    res.json(products);
});

// Add a new product
router.post('/', async (req, res) => {
    const product = new Product(req.body);
    await product.save();
    res.status(201).json(product);
});

module.exports = router;
```

2.2 Shopping Cart

Cart Model:

javascript

```javascript
// server/models/Cart.js
const mongoose = require('mongoose');

const cartSchema = new mongoose.Schema({
    userId: { type: mongoose.Schema.Types.ObjectId, ref: 'User', required: true },
    products: [
        {
            productId: { type: mongoose.Schema.Types.ObjectId, ref: 'Product' },
            quantity: { type: Number, default: 1 },
        },
    ],
});

module.exports = mongoose.model('Cart', cartSchema);
```

Cart Routes:

javascript

```javascript
// server/routes/cart.js
const express = require('express');
const Cart = require('../models/Cart');
const router = express.Router();

// Get user's cart
```

```
router.get('/:userId', async (req, res) => {
  const cart = await Cart.findOne({ userId: req.params.userId
}).populate('products.productId');
  res.json(cart);
});


// Add product to cart
router.post('/', async (req, res) => {
  const { userId, productId, quantity } = req.body;
  const cart = await Cart.findOneAndUpdate(
    { userId },
    { $push: { products: { productId, quantity } } },
    { new: true, upsert: true }
  );
  res.json(cart);
});


// Remove product from cart
router.delete('/:userId/:productId', async (req, res) => {
  const { userId, productId } = req.params;
  const cart = await Cart.findOneAndUpdate(
    { userId },
    { $pull: { products: { productId } } },
    { new: true }
  );
  res.json(cart);
});


module.exports = router;
```

2.3 Payment Integration

Install Stripe:

bash

npm install stripe

Stripe Checkout Route:

javascript

```javascript
// server/routes/checkout.js
const express = require('express');
const Stripe = require('stripe');
const router = express.Router();
const stripe = Stripe(process.env.STRIPE_SECRET_KEY);

// Create a payment session
router.post('/create-session', async (req, res) => {
  const { items } = req.body;

  const lineItems = items.map(item => ({
    price_data: {
      currency: 'usd',
      product_data: { name: item.name },
      unit_amount: item.price * 100,
    },
    quantity: item.quantity,
  }));

  const session = await stripe.checkout.sessions.create({
    payment_method_types: ['card'],
```

```
        line_items: lineItems,
        mode: 'payment',
        success_url: `${process.env.CLIENT_URL}/success`,
        cancel_url: `${process.env.CLIENT_URL}/cancel`,
    });

    res.json({ sessionId: session.id });
});


module.exports = router;
```

---

3. Front-End Development with React

3.1 Setting Up React

bash

```
npx create-react-app e-commerce-client
cd e-commerce-client
npm install axios react-router-dom
```

3.2 Directory Structure

css

```
e-commerce-client/
|
├── src/
|   ├── components/
|   ├── pages/
|   ├── App.js
```

```
|   └── index.js
```

3.3 Implementing Features

Product Listing:

javascript

```javascript
// src/pages/Products.js
import React, { useState, useEffect } from 'react';
import axios from 'axios';

function Products() {
  const [products, setProducts] = useState([]);

  useEffect(() => {
    axios.get('/api/products').then(response => setProducts(response.data));
  }, []);

  return (
    <div>
      {products.map(product => (
        <div key={product._id}>
          <h3>{product.name}</h3>
          <p>{product.description}</p>
          <p>${product.price}</p>
          <button>Add to Cart</button>
        </div>
      ))}
    </div>
  );
```

```
}
```

export default Products;

Checkout Page:

javascript

```
// src/pages/Checkout.js
import React from 'react';
import axios from 'axios';

function Checkout({ cart }) {
  const handleCheckout = async () => {
    const response = await axios.post('/api/checkout/create-session', { items: cart });
    window.location.href =
`https://checkout.stripe.com/pay/${response.data.sessionId}`;
  };

  return <button onClick={handleCheckout}>Proceed to Checkout</button>;
}

export default Checkout;
```

---

4. Deployment

4.1 Deploying the Back-End

Deploy the Node.js server on **Heroku**:

bash

git push heroku main

4.2 Deploying the Front-End

Deploy the React client on **Netlify**:

1. Build the React app:

   bash

   npm run build

2. Upload the build directory to Netlify.

---

5. Integrating Third-Party APIs

5.1 Shipping API Integration

Use services like **Shippo** or **EasyPost** to calculate shipping rates and manage shipments.

5.2 Real-Time Inventory

Sync inventory levels with an ERP or inventory management system.

Building an e-commerce website involves integrating front-end and back-end technologies to create a seamless user experience. With features like product catalogs, carts, and secure payment processing, this project equips developers with real-world skills in full-stack development. The next chapter will explore advanced data visualization techniques for full-stack applications.

Chapter 24: Building a Social Media Platform

Overview

Building a social media platform involves creating features like user profiles, real-time messaging, and notifications while ensuring dynamic and scalable data fetching. This chapter focuses on implementing these features and demonstrates how to use **GraphQL** for flexible and efficient data retrieval.

---

1. Project Setup

1.1 Back-End Setup

Use **Node.js** with **Express** and **Apollo Server** for the back end and **MongoDB** for the database.

Install Dependencies:

bash

```
mkdir social-media-platform
cd social-media-platform
npm init -y
npm install express mongoose apollo-server graphql bcryptjs jsonwebtoken cors dotenv
```

Directory Structure:

bash

```
social-media-platform/
|
├── server/
|   ├── models/
|   ├── resolvers/
|   ├── typeDefs/
|   ├── .env
|   ├── app.js
|   └── server.js
```

Server Configuration:

javascript

```javascript
// server/app.js
const express = require('express');
const { ApolloServer } = require('apollo-server-express');
const mongoose = require('mongoose');
const cors = require('cors');
const typeDefs = require('./typeDefs');
const resolvers = require('./resolvers');
require('dotenv').config();

const app = express();
app.use(cors());
app.use(express.json());

const server = new ApolloServer({ typeDefs, resolvers });

async function startServer() {
```

```
await server.start();
server.applyMiddleware({ app });

mongoose.connect(process.env.MONGO_URI, {
    useNewUrlParser: true,
    useUnifiedTopology: true,
}).then(() => console.log('MongoDB Connected'))
  .catch(err => console.error(err));

app.listen({ port: 4000 }, () => {
    console.log(`Server                running                at
http://localhost:4000${server.graphqlPath}`);
    });
}

startServer();
```

---

2. Core Features

2.1 User Profiles
User Model:

javascript

```
// server/models/User.js
const mongoose = require('mongoose');
const bcrypt = require('bcryptjs');

const userSchema = new mongoose.Schema({
```

```
    username: { type: String, required: true, unique: true },
    email: { type: String, required: true, unique: true },
    password: { type: String, required: true },
    bio: { type: String },
    profilePicture: { type: String },
});
```

```
// Hash password before saving
userSchema.pre('save', async function (next) {
    if (this.isModified('password')) {
        this.password = await bcrypt.hash(this.password, 10);
    }
    next();
});
```

```
module.exports = mongoose.model('User', userSchema);
```

GraphQL Type Definitions:

graphql

```
# server/typeDefs/user.js
const { gql } = require('apollo-server-express');

const userTypeDefs = gql`
    type User {
        id: ID!
        username: String!
        email: String!
        bio: String
        profilePicture: String
    }
```

```
input RegisterInput {
  username: String!
  email: String!
  password: String!
}

type Query {
  getUser(id: ID!): User
  getAllUsers: [User]
}

type Mutation {
  registerUser(input: RegisterInput): User
}
`;
```

module.exports = userTypeDefs;

GraphQL Resolvers:

javascript

```
// server/resolvers/user.js
const User = require('../models/User');

const userResolvers = {
  Query: {
    getUser: async (_, { id }) => await User.findById(id),
    getAllUsers: async () => await User.find(),
  },
  Mutation: {
```

```
    registerUser: async (_, { input }) => {
      const user = new User(input);
      await user.save();
      return user;
    },
  },
};


module.exports = userResolvers;
```

2.2 Real-Time Messaging
Message Model:

javascript

```
// server/models/Message.js
const mongoose = require('mongoose');

const messageSchema = new mongoose.Schema({
  sender: { type: mongoose.Schema.Types.ObjectId, ref: 'User', required: true },
  recipient: { type: mongoose.Schema.Types.ObjectId, ref: 'User', required: true },
  content: { type: String, required: true },
  timestamp: { type: Date, default: Date.now },
});


module.exports = mongoose.model('Message', messageSchema);
```

GraphQL Type Definitions:

graphql

```
# server/typeDefs/message.js
const { gql } = require('apollo-server-express');

const messageTypeDefs = gql`
  type Message {
    id: ID!
    sender: User!
    recipient: User!
    content: String!
    timestamp: String!
  }

  type Query {
    getMessages(senderId: ID!, recipientId: ID!): [Message]
  }

  type Mutation {
    sendMessage(senderId: ID!, recipientId: ID!, content: String!): Message
  }

  type Subscription {
    messageSent(recipientId: ID!): Message
  }
`;

module.exports = messageTypeDefs;
```

GraphQL Resolvers:

javascript

```
// server/resolvers/message.js
const { PubSub } = require('apollo-server-express');
const Message = require('../models/Message');
const pubsub = new PubSub();

const MESSAGE_SENT = 'MESSAGE_SENT';

const messageResolvers = {
  Query: {
    getMessages: async (_, { senderId, recipientId }) =>
      await Message.find({ $or: [{ sender: senderId, recipient: recipientId }, {
sender: recipientId, recipient: senderId }] }),
  },
  Mutation: {
    sendMessage: async (_, { senderId, recipientId, content }) => {
      const message = new Message({ sender: senderId, recipient: recipientId,
content });
      await message.save();
      pubsub.publish(MESSAGE_SENT, { messageSent: message });
      return message;
    },
  },
  Subscription: {
    messageSent: {
      subscribe:        (_,        {        recipientId        })        =>
pubsub.asyncIterator([MESSAGE_SENT]),
    },
  },
};
```

```javascript
module.exports = messageResolvers;
```

2.3 Notifications

Notification Model:

javascript

```javascript
// server/models/Notification.js
const mongoose = require('mongoose');

const notificationSchema = new mongoose.Schema({
    userId: { type: mongoose.Schema.Types.ObjectId, ref: 'User', required: true },
    content: { type: String, required: true },
    read: { type: Boolean, default: false },
    timestamp: { type: Date, default: Date.now },
});

module.exports = mongoose.model('Notification', notificationSchema);
```

Resolvers and Type Definitions: Create similar to Message.

---

3. Front-End Development with React

3.1 Setting Up React

bash

```bash
npx create-react-app social-media-client
cd social-media-client
npm install @apollo/client graphql react-router-dom
```

3.2 Integrating GraphQL with Apollo Client

javascript

```
// src/ApolloClient.js
import { ApolloClient, InMemoryCache } from '@apollo/client';

const client = new ApolloClient({
    uri: 'http://localhost:4000/graphql',
    cache: new InMemoryCache(),
});

export default client;
```

3.3 Example Feature: User Profile

Query Example:

javascript

```
import { gql, useQuery } from '@apollo/client';

const GET_USER = gql`
  query GetUser($id: ID!) {
    getUser(id: $id) {
      username
      bio
      profilePicture
    }
  }
`;
```

```
function UserProfile({ userId }) {
  const { loading, error, data } = useQuery(GET_USER, { variables: { userId }
});

  if (loading) return <p>Loading...</p>;
  if (error) return <p>Error: {error.message}</p>;

  const { username, bio, profilePicture } = data.getUser;

  return (
    <div>
      <h1>{username}</h1>
      <img src={profilePicture} alt={`${username}'s profile`} />
      <p>{bio}</p>
    </div>
  );
}
```

4. Deployment

4.1 Deploy Back-End

Deploy the Node.js server with GraphQL on **Heroku**.

4.2 Deploy Front-End

Deploy the React app on **Netlify** or **Vercel**.

Building a social media platform involves combining features like user profiles, real-time messaging, and notifications. Using **GraphQL** for dynamic data fetching ensures efficient and scalable communication between the client and server. This project provides hands-on experience with full-stack development and advanced features like subscriptions for real-time functionality.

Chapter 25: Final Capstone: Building a Scalable SaaS Application

Overview

In this final capstone project, we will combine all the concepts covered throughout the book to build a **Software-as-a-Service (SaaS)** application. This chapter focuses on designing a scalable, high-performance SaaS platform, with attention to best practices in scalability, performance, user experience, and maintainability.

---

1. Project Overview

1.1 Application Concept

SaaS Idea: Build a subscription-based project management tool with features like:

- **User authentication** and multi-tenant architecture.
- **Project and task management** with CRUD operations.
- **Real-time collaboration** using WebSockets.
- **Analytics dashboard** with dynamic data visualization.
- **Payment integration** for subscriptions.

1.2 Technology Stack

Layer	Technology
Front-End	React, Tailwind CSS
Back-End	Node.js, Express, Apollo Server (GraphQL)
Database	MongoDB (multi-tenant support)
Real-Time Features	Socket.io
Payments	Stripe
Hosting	AWS (Elastic Beanstalk, S3) or alternatives like Vercel and Netlify.

---

2. Architecture Design

2.1 Multi-Tenant Architecture

A multi-tenant architecture allows multiple users or organizations to use the application while maintaining data isolation.

Approaches:

1. **Database per Tenant:** Each tenant has its own database.
2. **Shared Database with Tenant Identifier:** A single database with tenant IDs to isolate data.

For this project:

- Use a **shared database** with tenant identifiers for simplicity and scalability.

2.2 Backend Structure

- Use GraphQL for flexible and efficient data queries.
- Design REST endpoints for payments and webhook handling.

2.3 Front-End Structure

- Modularize React components for reusability.
- Use state management libraries like Redux or Context API for global state.

---

3. Back-End Implementation

3.1 Setting Up the Server
Install Dependencies:

bash

```
mkdir saas-app
cd saas-app
npm init -y
```

npm install express mongoose apollo-server graphql bcryptjs jsonwebtoken socket.io stripe cors dotenv

Server Configuration:

javascript

```
// server/app.js
const express = require('express');
const { ApolloServer } = require('apollo-server-express');
const mongoose = require('mongoose');
const cors = require('cors');
require('dotenv').config();

const typeDefs = require('./typeDefs');
const resolvers = require('./resolvers');
const { createServer } = require('http');
const { Server } = require('socket.io');

const app = express();
app.use(cors());
app.use(express.json());

mongoose.connect(process.env.MONGO_URI, {
    useNewUrlParser: true,
    useUnifiedTopology: true,
}).then(() => console.log('MongoDB Connected'))
  .catch(err => console.error(err));

const apolloServer = new ApolloServer({ typeDefs, resolvers });
apolloServer.applyMiddleware({ app });
```

```javascript
const httpServer = createServer(app);
const io = new Server(httpServer);

io.on('connection', (socket) => {
  console.log('User connected');
  socket.on('disconnect', () => console.log('User disconnected'));
});

httpServer.listen(4000, () => {
  console.log(`Server                              running                    at
http://localhost:4000${apolloServer.graphqlPath}`);
});
```

3.2 Multi-Tenant Database Design

User Model:

javascript

```javascript
// server/models/User.js
const mongoose = require('mongoose');
const bcrypt = require('bcryptjs');

const userSchema = new mongoose.Schema({
  tenantId: { type: String, required: true }, // Tenant identifier
  username: { type: String, required: true },
  email: { type: String, required: true },
  password: { type: String, required: true },
});

userSchema.pre('save', async function (next) {
```

```
  if (this.isModified('password')) {
    this.password = await bcrypt.hash(this.password, 10);
  }
  next();
});
```

```
module.exports = mongoose.model('User', userSchema);
```

Project and Task Models:

javascript

```javascript
// server/models/Project.js
const mongoose = require('mongoose');

const projectSchema = new mongoose.Schema({
  tenantId: { type: String, required: true },
  name: { type: String, required: true },
  description: { type: String },
  tasks: [
    {
      name: { type: String, required: true },
      completed: { type: Boolean, default: false },
    },
  ],
});

module.exports = mongoose.model('Project', projectSchema);
```

3.3 Real-Time Collaboration

Socket.io Integration: Enable real-time updates for tasks:

javascript

```javascript
io.on('connection', (socket) => {
    console.log('User connected to real-time collaboration');

    socket.on('updateTask', (data) => {
        io.emit('taskUpdated', data);
    });
});
```

Client Integration:

javascript

```javascript
import { io } from 'socket.io-client';

const socket = io('http://localhost:4000');

socket.on('taskUpdated', (data) => {
    console.log('Task updated:', data);
});
```

3.4 Payment Integration

Stripe Checkout Integration:

javascript

```javascript
// server/routes/payments.js
const express = require('express');
```

```
const Stripe = require('stripe');
const router = express.Router();
const stripe = Stripe(process.env.STRIPE_SECRET_KEY);

router.post('/create-checkout-session', async (req, res) => {
  const session = await stripe.checkout.sessions.create({
    payment_method_types: ['card'],
    line_items: req.body.items.map(item => ({
      price_data: {
        currency: 'usd',
        product_data: { name: item.name },
        unit_amount: item.price * 100,
      },
      quantity: item.quantity,
    })),
    mode: 'subscription',
    success_url: `${process.env.CLIENT_URL}/success`,
    cancel_url: `${process.env.CLIENT_URL}/cancel`,
  });

  res.json({ sessionId: session.id });
});

module.exports = router;
```

4. Front-End Implementation

4.1 React App Setup

bash

```
npx create-react-app saas-client
cd saas-client
npm install @apollo/client graphql axios socket.io-client stripe
```

4.2 Key Features

Dashboard Component:

javascript

```javascript
// src/components/Dashboard.js
import React from 'react';

function Dashboard({ projects }) {
  return (
    <div>
      {projects.map(project => (
        <div key={project.id}>
          <h3>{project.name}</h3>
          <p>{project.description}</p>
        </div>
      ))}
    </div>
  );
}
```

export default Dashboard;

Real-Time Task Updates:

javascript

```
// src/components/Task.js
import React, { useEffect, useState } from 'react';
import { io } from 'socket.io-client';

const socket = io('http://localhost:4000');

function Task({ task }) {
  const [completed, setCompleted] = useState(task.completed);

  useEffect(() => {
    socket.on('taskUpdated', (updatedTask) => {
      if (updatedTask.id === task.id) {
        setCompleted(updatedTask.completed);
      }
    });
  }, [task]);

  const toggleComplete = () => {
    const updatedTask = { ...task, completed: !completed };
    socket.emit('updateTask', updatedTask);
  };

  return (
    <div>
      <p>{task.name}</p>
      <button onClick={toggleComplete}>
        {completed ? 'Mark Incomplete' : 'Mark Complete'}
      </button>
    </div>
```

```
  );
}
```

export default Task;

---

5. Deployment

5.1 Hosting Back-End
Use **AWS Elastic Beanstalk** or **Heroku**.

5.2 Hosting Front-End
Deploy the React app to **Netlify** or **Vercel**.

---

6. Best Practices

1. **Scalability:**
   - Use a load balancer and auto-scaling groups for high traffic.
   - Optimize database queries for multi-tenancy.
2. **Security:**
   - Use HTTPS for secure communication.
   - Implement role-based access control (RBAC) for user permissions.
3. **Performance Optimization:**

- o Enable caching for frequently accessed data (e.g., Redis).
- o Use lazy loading for components and assets.

This SaaS capstone project integrates concepts of multi-tenant architecture, real-time collaboration, secure payment systems, and modern UI/UX practices. By following these steps, you will build a scalable and maintainable SaaS platform, showcasing your full-stack development expertise.

www.ingramcontent.com/pod-product-compliance
Lightning Source LLC
LaVergne TN
LVHW051438050326
832903LV00030BD/3146